The Wheels
of
Society

The Wheels
of
Society

Its Assembly, Performance and Emotion

A. C. B. Wilson

QUARTET BOOKS

First published in 2021 by Quartet Books Limited
A member of the Namara Group
27 Goodge Street, London, W1T 2LD

A catalogue record for this book
is available from the British Library

ISBN 9780704374829

Typeset by Avon DataSet Ltd, Arden Court, Alcester, Warwickshire

Printed and bound in Great Britain by
TJ Books Limited, Padstow, Cornwall

In memory of John Gibson

CONTENTS

PREFACE

Ever since I can remember I have always wanted to know how society works, if only to learn how to behave properly.

The idea elaborated in these pages first came to me while struggling to defend myself against the accusation of corporate greed. It was in 1997 during a bike-ride round the coast of Ireland. My companion and very dear old friend John Gibson, a well-known salmon biologist, had repeatedly wrestled me to defeat, and yet I knew we business executives were not evil.

I published a preliminary sketch of the idea in 2007 when my book *The Universe on a Bicycle* was published by Elliott and Thompson.

By the spring of 2019, the main elements had fallen into place. The last one in was about the power of social, or corporate, emotion; about how emotion functions as a safety valve when a group needs to be reassembled. It dawned on me that any ideas about how society works must remain boringly academic, uninterestingly intellectual, unless they can accommodate the irrational function of social emotion: panic, pride, shame, sorrow and triumph.

As I write this in June 2020, the saga of the Covid 19 'flu pandemic is a chilling example of the power of social emotion. Emotion was the missing piece; it dosed all the others with an everyday infusion of reality. At last it was time to shut the ideas-door which had been letting in a tumble of fascinating perceptions. The time to publish had arrived. The central theme is called assembly-and-performance thinking; often referred to here as A&PT.

INTRODUCTION

Sociology should be able to tell us how society works, but it seems confused. For example, we do not appear to have a workable explanation of corporate greed; it is widely disliked and yet we really have no intelligent, workably scientific answer to it. So, I wanted to rethink the basics.

To an almost pathetic degree we rely on society for everything we need: food, self-protection and breeding. Without it none of us, neither the prime minister nor the fisherman, could survive a month. Personally, I would perish in two weeks. Human society is made up of groups of cooperating individuals arranged in an untidy, rough-and-tumble hierarchy. It is an amazing set-up, a game of 'survive and prosper' in which everybody has a part to play.

As individuals we work in cycles. Our myriad performances, the everyday things we do alone, like boiling an egg, always cycle through three types of function:

....

1. We REVIEW the situation:

2. We PLAN how to do the job:

3

3. We DO it, and then:

1. We review again and repeat. It is a trial-and-error cycle. That's my first point.

....

My second point, and here's the thing, is that every group, including family, multinational corporation and nation, obeys exactly this same performance logic as do individuals; I will argue that over the long term there is no other way. Each group, driven by corporate ambition, cycles repeatedly, and with purpose, through these same three types of function. If this is true, we may be able to build on it to solve the enigma of society, to describe its mechanism, and that is the purpose of this book.

These arguments, I lump them together as 'assembly and perform-ance thinking', come under sociology; they are easily crowded out by economics and philosophy which between them dominate the world stage on which our political debates take place. Any new ideas about human prosperity must fight hard against sound bites like, 'it's the economy stupid.'

But economists ignore the everyday obvious: that groups are more significant actors in our lives than individuals acting alone. And philosophers are not very realistic either; they commonly disregard the lessons of natural selection and when pushed they retreat behind obscure words into introspection and homo-centricity. Economists and philosophers have been unable to solve the antisocial problems of corporate greed and genocide, and neither discipline can accommodate the emotions which trigger so much of our social behaviour, rough and ready as it unfortunately is.

To get a hearing, assembly and performance thinking must make a robust case for itself. This has inevitably meant jousting, like Don Quixote, with some well-established windmills. And I do that. But I most certainly do not want to rubbish economics or philosophy, or even to regret capitalism. It would be crazy to disregard the tremendous social value of the treasury models with which we fine-tune our economies. Without them we would have little protection against runaway bankers' gambling sprees; against 'boom and bust'. My purpose in tilting at economics and philosophy is simply to clear some intellectual space, so as to examine the mechanisms of human society, and to try and see how they actually do work.

I claim that we should first think about how, despite individual selfishness, groups can assemble in the first place? Furthermore, how can it be possible for these groups to be the independent self-motivating units which they clearly are? Then, but only then, we can begin to think about how each group actually performs. In logic, these two are totally distinct questions. Assembly is about the principles of natural selection, whereas performance iterates a feedback loop.

These arguments are based on evolutionary biology. Despite the massive obstacle of individual selfishness, Darwin called it 'the struggle for existence', cooperation is such a successful strategy that it has evolved many times, independently, throughout the animal kingdom. It occurs in the slime-mould and other colonial creatures like the siphonophores, also in insects, fish, birds and mammals. Even certain microbes cooperate, and when they do, the basics of assembly and performance still hold good, as Stuart West of Oxford University, writing in *Current Biology* (2007), demonstrated.

Philosophy is all about the strictly personal, introspective, speculations which we all occasionally make within our own minds about consciousness, existence, knowledge and reality. But cooperating groups clearly do not have minds at all. They are much too primitive to speculate introspectively; they cannot philosophise. This means that the venerable techniques of philosophy cannot apply to the way groups 'think'; the techniques of human introspection just are not relevant. And yet it is undeniable that groups, as units, reason things out; they perform something, independent of any one leader, which amounts to thinking.

To flip this thought round: though jellyfish may not have minds, they are not exactly mindless. This is a 'quasi-mind' observation which can be taken a fascinating step further by the colonial creatures, the Portuguese man o' war is one, in which it is hard to deny that the colony, which eats, protects itself and breeds *as a unit*, does behave as though it had a primitive mind; it orchestrates its own purposeful trial-and-error behaviour. There lies the enigma of society: how does it work? How do the members of a social colony work together? Similarly, the trial-and-error workings of human social groups, a road-repairing gang say, or a village cider-making committee, all follow recognisably recurring, purposeful, patterns of behaviour. So too do beehives, ant colonies and termite mounds. In each case the assembled group has a job to do; it is not exactly mindless; each group is self-motivated. These quasi-mind workings are at the very heart of the assembly and performance thinking promoted here.

Support for this way of thinking comes from simulation. When a group task looks like being a big deal, we often simulate it first. Military strategy is a good example: first you recruit, or *assemble*, then you fight, or *perform*. How well or badly the battle goes then feeds back into your ability to recruit, and vice versa. War games simulate the outcomes of critical decisions. Other popular simulations include those addictive teenagers' video games which pit competing sports clubs against each other, simulating the knife-edge balancing act of the manager. *FIFA*, which simulates football, is a good example, but my favourite is *hitwicketcricket.com* which simulates competition in the Indian Premier League.

In Part 1 I have tried to defend these sometimes challenging ideas by denying the hubris promoted so brilliantly by Plato and others, and by distinguishing, with child-like innocence, between 'things' and 'non-things'.

A Bike-Ride

After cycling round the rugged coast of Ireland with my old friend John, I published a breezy diary of our trip (*The Universe on a Bicycle*, by Tony Wilson, Elliott & Thompson, 2007). It was all about the people we met and the magnificent rain-soaked scenery. A recurring theme was the plight of the Atlantic salmon.

John Gibson and I had been at Trinity College, Dublin together. He eventually became a professor of salmon ecology in Canada, and he kept on pointing out how big business, an evil monster with its hydroelectric schemes and irresponsible agricultural practices, had more or less wiped out the Atlantic salmon throughout our beloved island. John reminded us of this at each of the great rivers we crossed; the Lee, Shannon, Corrib, Moy, Erne, Foyle, Bann, Boyne, Liffey, Slaney, Barrow-Nore-Suir and the Blackwater. We had rowed together in the TCD senior eight on many of them. Ireland is quite small, but it rains a lot and the rivers are mighty.

But my whole career had been in industry. I had been financial controller in several big English corporations. My calling was under attack and I had little or no defence against John's contempt for industry. I had to admit that we businessmen were ruthlessly greedy for success and yet I personally knew that the companies I had worked for certainly were not evil. There was a problem there, no doubt about it, and many of the things we chatted about as we pedalled along roused an interest in how actually society does work. What are its mechanisms?

It seemed important to start at rock bottom. I reasoned, and John agreed, that the human is no more and no less than an animal and a highly cooperative one at that, and so if I could learn more about how cooperation has evolved in animals, it ought to be possible to work out how corporate greed itself might have evolved.

The question we tackled boiled down to this: 'How did natural selection evolve the misuse of power?' Animals and natural selection were always at John's fingertips, so his angle was increasingly promising.

The Great Prophets

After that bike-ride I spent years dipping into books and learned papers looking for anybody who might help; anybody who might have explained how society works. The two groups most relevant seemed to be philosophers, the ancient scholars of mankind, and sociologists, the modern scholars of society. Evolutionary biology gradually became the most promising source for answers.

The great prophets Confucius, Buddha, Moses, Christ and Mohammed were essentially sociologists. Most impressive of all were the ancient Greeks: Socrates, the grandfather of sociology, Plato the dreamer and Aristotle the realist; they penetrated further than almost anyone before or since. The ancient Romans seemed to have little to contribute. The medieval Arab scholars, including Omar Khayyam, Ibn Rashd *aka* Averroes, Ibn Khaldun and Avicenna, were brilliant, especially in medicine and astronomy. But my research suggested that all these men, never women by the way, took it for granted that mankind stands alone, apart from animals, which, being a committed Darwinian since childhood, I could not accept.

Only a minority of social thinkers have ever treated the human as a mere animal. This has meant that the great prophets have been left free to fantasise about humanoid Gods. They saw no need to ground their beliefs and theories on our animal nature. They were not obliged to integrate their teaching about society with the group intelligence that has always been observed in ants, hyenas and wolves. Their universally homocentric starting point has excused every single one of the ancients, Buddha to Jesus and Confucius to Mohammed, from delving into the animal workings of human society.

After these ancient writings, the field of sociology dramatically opens up. Charles Darwin has only been recognised reluctantly by philosophers and sociologists. The huge number of learned articles saying Darwin was wrong is a fitting testament to his greatness. The big names before him include Bacon, Descartes, Rousseau, Mandeville, Kant, Hobbes, Locke and Hume. Then after Darwin came the great modern sociologists: Comte, Durkheim, Marx, and Weber, and after them we have had a series of twentieth-century schools of sociology.

Wikipedia and the Circular Argument

Researching for about twenty years, I accumulated books, textbooks, specialised dictionaries and learned articles. And I used Wikipedia. My excuse for this is that Wikipedia is tremendously helpful for following up trails and cross-referencing gems of 'knowledge' (slippery word), while you accumulate and browse your source material.

The question: 'How did natural selection evolve the misuse of power?' may be loaded with assumptions but it is clear and simple, and if you are driven along by an idea of what you are looking for, Wikipedia can help with the job of avoiding side-issues. Though I respect the intellectual integrity of those who are suspicious of its 'confirmation bias' trap, Wikipedia has greatly eased my search through masses of scholarly material.

Like an opening batsman in test cricket, if your purpose is clear, Wikipedia helps you to ignore the bouncers. For example: if a scholar – let us say Kant – is clearly striving to justify his belief in a superior power, his thoughts can be ignored in my search for the evolutionary origin of corporate greed, because a belief in God is incompatible with the doctrine of evolution by natural selection.

I refer to the argument of the circular fallacy several times in this book; it is an error in which the scholar begins by assuming, as given, the conclusion he is trying to end up with. It is a common logical mistake, it comes in many forms, and is often difficult to spot.

A good example underpins Y. N. Harari's *Sapiens – A Brief History of Humankind*, published by Vintage in 2011. In this otherwise excellent history book Harari constantly assumes as given the prior existence of human society. He does this without probing the evolution of cooperation which is, after all, the basis of every animal society: slime-mould, siphonophore, ant, naked mole-rat and human. This is no mere quibble because, though it does not invalidate the bulk of the history he writes, this fallacy leads Harari into the common failure to recognise the function of culture in all social mammals. It blinds Harari to the logical difference between the mechanisms of social assembly and social performance. This circular argument allows Harari to treat *Homo sapiens* as a special animal, standing apart from all others in the animal kingdom. Harari's *sapiens* is assumed to be an animal with a special pre-existing ability to assemble into cooperating groups. *Sapiens* is a co-operator therefore he can cooperate.

The arguments I put forward in this book continually chip away at the misconceptions arising from this fallacy: the fallacy of the social circular argument.

Philosophy and sociology both deal with cooperation, but when each subject is stripped like a Russian doll back to first principles, it becomes clear that Harari is not on his own. Both these disciplines usually take the prior existence of society for granted. So, any claims they make about the evolution of cooperation usually amount to circular argument. To say that 'society thrives because altruism confers a competitive advantage' explains how altruism can persist in a species but not how it arose in the first place. It is the fallacy which underlies all today's great religions. This fallacy also applies to any claim that game theory explains the origin of social behaviour. Quite simply, solitaries do not play games so, though game theory is excellent at analysing how altruism survives in a social species, it cannot explain how sociality arose in the first place.

The Inspiration for Assembly and Performance Thinking

Cooperating creatures must, it is obvious, be able to switch their modes of behaviour effortlessly from individual to team player and from team player to group-as-a-unit. It was while I was trying to understand how these transitions can work, that I noticed there is a clear difference in logic between assembling to do a job and then doing it. The one is explained by Darwin's natural selection; the other depends on a feedback-control loop. It therefore seemed sensible to study them separately, and right enough this became a fruitful line of research.

The Misuse of Human Power

Sociology is typically a pathology, a science of remedies. The misuse of power has always been its driving force. From Buddha to Marx, Socrates to Mohammed, Jesus to Kant, Abraham to Bentham, the underlying question has always been human violence. That's why we do sociology: we want to understand the regularities of social breakdown. Why do we so often resort to warfare, slavery, oppression, dictatorship, corruption, rebellion and corporate greed? Why do we ignore the looming danger of climate change? Why have we persecuted the magnificent Atlantic salmon in Ireland to near-extinction?

The drivers of religion and sociology have almost always been social breakdown and the misuse of human power. The result of this is that several of the less spectacular mechanisms of society tend to be neglected. One example is the interplay between irrational and rational *group* mentalities, this is another recurring theme in this book.

The search for the causes of social breakdown is still on. Modern sociologists who have shaped our understanding of human violence include Emile Durkheim with his 'Anomie', Marx with his proletariat-capitalism dialectic, Weber with his 'Verstehen', Talcott Parsons with his AGIL, John Rawls with his 'Justice as Fairness' and Pierre Bourdieu with his 'Structure and Agency'. Today there is still a feeling that it must be possible to find the answer to the misuse of human power, but nobody has yet put their finger on it. It is still an enigma. I will explain below why I believe Durkheim was closest of them all.

The Quasi-Mind Pulls the Strings

When society is running smoothly nobody outside universities bothers much about it. People get on with life: eating OK, adequately housed and raising families. Women may not always be heard but they have always been listened to. Men strut about pretending they're in charge. It's only when trouble threatens that power becomes an issue. Until then nobody, other than politicians and sociologists, thinks very deeply about power.

When social breakdown threatens in family, business, tribe or nation, then the women call for action and the men take over. But how should we exercise social power? How can we prevent its misuse? Who is to wield it?

As J. J. Rousseau once said there is a general will which is different from and more powerful than the votes of the elected majority. In this book I refer to this general will as the quasi-mind of the group; it's the self-motivating spirit – I avoid the word 'agent' – which presides over and orchestrates the behaviour of the group and which either caused it to assemble in the first place or which maintains its energy.

Being a group manifestation, this quasi-mind is only capable of rudimentary brainwork.

This primitive self-motivating quasi-mind seems to be where social power lies and, as Le Bon pointed out, when roused it is essentially irrational, instinctive and emotional; here is how he described it:

> Under certain given circumstances, and only under those circumstances, an agglomeration of men presents new characteristics very different from those of the individuals composing it. The sentiments and ideas of all the persons in the gathering take one and the same direction, and their conscious personality vanishes. A collective mind is formed, doubtless transitory, but presenting very clearly defined characteristics. The gathering has become what, in the absence of a better expression, I will call an organised crowd, or, if the term is considered preferable, a psychological crowd. It forms a single being and is subject to the law of the mental unity of crowds.
>
> Le Bon, *The Crowd*, Dover Books

Much of the time the group mind hums along steadily in the background but when trouble brews in family, corporation or nation, emotion injects social electricity, deciding that something has to be done. Then the rational principle steps in and tries to do it. So, power seems to reside in the self-motivating quasi-mind, or will, of the group, and the daily exercise of power seems to be shared in a dialectical give-and-take between the emotional and rational elements of society.

star = plan it, whirl = do it, book = review it

Lux, Lumen, Illuminatio

In medieval France, the Abbe Suger (1081–1151) abbot of the Basilica at Saint Denis expounded the theological theory of light. External every-day natural light he said was *Lux*. Then as it passed through the stained glass of a cathedral window it was transformed into *Lumen*, the holy light of God. Finally, when it was perceived by the righteous, boosted perhaps by a fanfare from the organ pipes, it conferred transcendental understanding; called *Illuminatio*. This idea is not only a wondrous lens through which we can appreciate medieval art, it is still a powerful metaphor today for the way in which painting can use external light to transform everyday reality into inner illumination; first it's out there in the street, next you take a deeply respectful look, finally bingo – you've got it!

This book is similarly divided into in three parts: PART 1 Social Reality describes what we all see in daily life. PART 2 Social Theory expounds Assembly and Performance Thinking, it accommodates emotion and it claims to explain the mechanisms of society. PART 3 lists the Illuminations, examples and solutions which are lit up by the idea.

PART 1 Social Reality Is Descriptive

It tries to establish what really does go on in society – how does it work actually? Social life is looked at through the perspectives of first a child, then a student, an apprentice, a mother, an employee and finally a senior citizen. The great sociologists are reviewed in PART 1, but because the aim is to refresh our grasp of social reality, I have side-stepped the conventional format for sociology-writing. Textbooks usually tell the story chronologically, reviewing the great sociologists in sequence from ancient times to the present day. The alternative, the 'life-stages' approach used here, may allow us to relate classical and modern social thought more directly, autobiographically even, to our own personal realities. After all, personal experience is the only possible way anybody, even a learned professor, can take in the realities of social life. There is none other available to you or me. Everything we get from conversations, books and TV may be information but it's not *real* in this sense, it is second-hand reality.

There are more questions than answers in PART 1. And the big one underlying them all like a volcanic fault is this enigma: 'How did natural selection evolve the misuse of power?'

PART 2 Assembly and Performance Thinking, Is Theoretical

Assembly and performance thinking offers a coherent set of reality-answers to the questions left dangling in PART 1. These apply the principle of natural selection to an analysis of how human cooperation is achieved. The rule of three is central here. This is the triangular, trial-and-error, 'review > plan > execute' cycle which unfolds the logic of a performance optimising loop. This loop, unless it is overwhelmed by the exciting force of emotion, orchestrates all animal social behaviour. The rule of three describes a persistent but weak force motivating all mammal groups including human societies.

It is not as complicated as it sounds, and while researching, I sometimes wondered if the Christian triumvirate of Father, Son, and Holy Ghost may have been an intuitive recognition by the ancients of the rule of three. That obscure doctrine certainly did puzzle me when I was a teenager. Triumvirates are political structures in which social performance is orchestrated by three people or agents in a power sharing arrangement. There are many examples of such structures and a good one is in the three cosmic functions of Hindu: The Trimurti of Brahma the creator, Vishnu the preserver and Shiva the destroyer. Another is the doctrine that political power should be separated into legislature, executive and judiciary. But none of the triumvirates I could find are able to bind or lock themselves into a working mechanism: the inter-relations of the triumvirate are never satisfactorily explained.

My claim is that I may be unearthing the workings of a logical lock here which has never been noticed before. I suggest that every power-sharing triumvirate can be locked into a working mechanism if the three powers can be made mutually trumping. This universal logic underlies all animal social performance, a claim I elaborate in PART 2.

There are echoes of Darwin in PART 2. These arguments are 'unscientific' in the sense that they cannot be replicated by experiment or falsified on the laboratory bench of real life. But this is also true of natural selection, it cannot be proved either; the fact that natural selection has never yet been falsified does not amount to scientific proof. Both natural selection and the assembly and performance thinking promoted here explain why things happened the way they did. But neither can predict what is going to happen next.

PART 3 Illuminates

It lists two sets of social issues which are lit up, as by the abbé Suger's stained glass, by assembly and performance thinking. The first is a collection of politico-social notes. These are practical suggestions about various social issues including law-making, bullying, psychiatry, the balance of powers and more. The second set of illuminations consists of philosophical insights regarding bureaucracy, culture, the nature of God, the structure/agency question and more.

The illuminations in PART 3 help to defend and promote assembly and performance thinking; some are chillingly bleak, others optimistic; the claim is that their common origin adds a ring of truth to the whole idea.

What's the Story?

OK, so what is the story? Well it's simply this: that recognising a clear difference between the way people assemble to get things done, and the way they actually do them might lead us to a better understanding of how society works, and if not exactly how to control it, at least how to diagnose its diseases; this would be somewhat like using ecology to maintain the health of a rainforest. If you can understand the principals involved, then you are better able to avoid mistakes. The story can be summarised as follows.

Humans like all animals must acquire energy, protect themselves and reproduce. These are the necessities of life.

Being a co-operating animal, we *assemble* to do these things in groups: farms, businesses, armies, criminal gangs, working parties, villages. These groups have rudimentary minds of their own, or quasi-minds.

Society is seen here as a rough-and-tumble of groups spontaneously, or serendipitously, arranged in a hierarchy.

The rule of three, 'review > plan > execute', describes a triumvirate; it's a mutually trumping feedback control loop. It is the default logic at the beating heart of society's mechanisms. This rule, which orchestrates group *performance*, wields a weak but persistent force.

Emotion is the opposite. It applies a strong but ephemeral force. Panic or disgust can destroy a group. A new group can then immediately be assembled if necessary.

As in the job of a football-club manager, there is reciprocal interplay between *assembly* and *performance*. Effective performance enhances his ability to attract star players; poor performance makes this more difficult.

So, there is a fundamental difference in logic between the mechanisms of group *assembly* and group *performance*. And that is why I often refer to this story as 'assembly and performance thinking'.

Human self-importance, or hubris, prevents us from seeing these truths. God is a simple, powerful and understandable idea invented to explain the group quasi-mind. Quite simply religion turns the quasi-mind into a person to be worshipped. This reveals God to be a fallacy based on human self-importance. It should have been exposed for all to see by Darwin's *Origin of Species*, but God still rules OK all over much of the world.

Reverse Trumping

When a group or society is running smoothly, the performance functions – plan, execute and review – trump each other. Each trumps the next in a cybernetic feedback control loop. But if at any time one function goes into reverse, trumping backwards as it were, this gums up the works.

There are three types. One is rebellion, in which 'planning' reverses into and disregards 'reviewing', as in the French Revolution. Another is autocracy, or dictatorship, in which 'execution', no play on words intended, reverses into 'planning', as in Nazi Germany. And the third, sclerosis, happens when excessive formality in 'reviewing' hampers executive response, again interfering with the smooth cycling of the loop.

Thus, the social damage caused by reverse trumping supports

assembly and performance thinking. By harnessing emotion reverse trumping can cause social breakdown, even violence as it upsets the smooth cycling of the loop.

Emil Durkheim, at the end of his book *The Division of Labour in Society* identified three 'forms' of society in which social solidarity gets weakened; he called them 'The Anomic Division of Labour', 'The Forced Division of Labour' and 'Another Abnormal Form'. Durkheim's abnormal forms correspond almost perfectly to the three types of reverse trumping proposed here. The concept of reverse trumping, like Yang reinforcing Yin in Chinese philosophy, negatively confirms assembly and performance thinking, this is discussed in more detail at the end of Part 2.

The rule of three amounts to a 'weak force'. It is not a rigid mechanism. Instead it amounts to a weak but persistent social force applying to both individual and group performance. In the long run it gives a group the advantage of rational behaviour over competing groups which ignore it. In any particular encounter failure to follow the rule may be marginal, but over repeated episodes of competition with rival groups, this failure can be cumulative.

This rule applies to individual performance as well as to groups. But since the minds of individuals are very much quicker and more flexible than the more rudimentary quasi-minds of groups, adherence to the cycle is very much more important for groups than it is for individuals. In individuals, quick-reacting intuition, the first cousin of emotion, can cut corners. A standing army uses set structures and procedures, but a terrorist cell or group can, in Mohammed Ali's wonderful words, 'float like a butterfly and sting like a bee'.

Irrationality versus Rationality

A word here about irrationality: The tension between the rational and the irrational appears often in this book. In PART 1 it complicates the mother's view of reality, likewise the worker's and the senior citizen's, and in PART 2 we see how irrational excitement can use the overwhelming power of emotion to disrupt, reassemble or even destroy a social group. My aim is not to explain irrationality but simply to treat it with great respect as a sensitive nerve which crackles constantly in our social lives. It acts like a safety-valve. Irrationality can be vital for success. It is triggered by emotions such as fear, sexual attraction and hatred. As Hamlet, Prince of Denmark, said in his eponymous play, 'My words [rational] fly up, my thoughts [irrational] remain below.'

E. R. Dodds, writing in his *Greeks and the Irrational,* is one of many scholars who have written fascinatingly on the subject. Here is what it says on the back cover of his 1951 edition:

> Greek culture has long been identified with the triumph of rationalism. The role of primitive and irrational forces in Greek society has been largely glossed over or neglected even when it was obviously touched on by the Greeks themselves. In this volume, armed with analytical weapons of modern anthropology and psychology, Professor Dodds asks, 'Why should we attribute to the ancient Greeks an immunity from "primitive" modes of thought which we do not find in any society open to our direct observation?'

Who Should Run the Show?

OK so who should be running the show? Should we be governed by pointy-headed intellectuals like Gordon Brown or by gut-feeling demagogues like Margaret Thatcher and Donald Trump? The rational mind works at the cutting edge of sociology, philosophy, science and technology, but the irrational has a hotline to panic, joy, sadness, common sense, triumph and hysteria; these are powerful group motivators. Being more directly, more viscerally, linked to the universal life-imperatives, eating, self-protection and breeding, the irrational effortlessly trumps the rational when group wellbeing is in doubt. The social reaction to the recent Coronavirus epidemic is an excellent demonstration of group rationality being overwhelmed by panic when wellbeing is in doubt. Car accidents kill many more people than the flu, but we hardly notice road death statistics in our daily behaviour. Any social theory must be able to deal with surges of excitement or floods of emotional energy.

This question of who should run the show is dealt with in PART 2 and also at the end of PART 3.

Sociology Disappoints

The problem confronting the student of sociology today is that although there are some excellent scholars active all over the world, and despite the fact that laptops enable them all to read and discuss each other's work, there seems to be no recognised consensus about how society works. This of course is not unusual in human affairs; for example, it takes time, often decades, before the art market settles the league table of all-time greatest painters, and the electronic revolution now careering like a tidal wave through society, shaking cultural norms, makes it particularly difficult to agree the league table of today's leading sociological theories. But no excuses can quell the ancient and ever-present feeling that human society does function according to universal patterns; it's just that they haven't been discovered yet. In other words, we do still sense the possibility of finding a universally applicable body of social theory.

In his introduction to *Handbook of Contemporary Sociological Theory* (2016), Professor Seth Abrutyn of the University of British Columbia writes about the muddle sociology is in at the moment, lamenting that there is no consensus:

> I have also come to recognise the need for a coherent language and, as I have seen from the reaction of students exhausted from being presented one vision of social reality after another from one class to the next, [I recognise the need for] a relatively coherent view of the social universe.

Many modern sociologists avoid universal theories altogether, preferring to tackle specific, often minority, problems; others stray into utopia. What seems to be missing is an accepted core of social theory. Abrutyn ends his introduction with a rallying cry:

Ultimately, the discipline is due for a paradigm shift. If theory is a specialisation, then we need to resuscitate and support theorists in journals, professorial appointments, and in training; if theory is the backbone of a social science, then we need to begin to teach theory as a set of principles that sociologists can deploy in developing research. This *Handbook* is one small step forward, inspired by the desire to unite sociologists under a common umbrella that *does not* dissuade creativity, the pursuit of understudied problems, or the continued development of theory. A society or community, rather than an association, is more likely to cooperate in an effort to push sociology into the twenty-first century and make our discipline one that is consulted when politicians, economic leaders, community organisers, and the like have problems they need help solving.

Hubris: A Disease of the Group Mind, and the Oozlum Bird

Self-Importance is one of the things that gets in the way of clear thinking about society. This is natural; the starting point when we wonder about ourselves is exactly that: it is ourselves. From there it is unfortunately, easy to believe ourselves to be all-important in the grand scheme of things. All the great religions put the human gloriously at the centre of the universe. Buddha decried this misleading tendency, so did several of the ancient Greeks. A major theme in Homer's epic poems, the *Iliad* and the *Odyssey*, was the folly of human impertinence towards the Gods; it was called hubris. Plato however, despite these warnings, built his gloriously homocentric cosmology, described in the *Timaeus* on what Protagoras before him had referred to as, 'Man the measure of all things'. This view was accepted without challenge in approved versions of Judaism, Christianity and Islam. Georg Hegel, a Christian writing in 1821, in his seminal *Philosophy of Mind*, went even further. He said, 'Man is not sharply distinct from God but rises to God over the course of history.' This is hubris for us, in the raw.

This fallacy does not occur when individuals think about themselves; it seldom occurs to one person that he or she might be the greatest creature on earth. That is madness, it's deluded thinking; you can be locked up for it. However, the requirement of group solidarity imposes upon its members a strong and loyal belief in the importance of the group; of itself.

That is how the quasi-mind of the group works. It is a short but false step from there to: 'WE are the greatest.' This attitude is then fed back, with banners and speeches by priests and politicians, into the individual person's psyche, consolidating the belief in the uniqueness of mankind. This very word 'mankind' is a giveaway here; it has a masculine, chest-beating ring to it.

Hubris is entirely natural; it is essentially a group thing, but it inhibits clear thinking about the mechanisms of society. I blame hubris for leading us into the circular fallacy that society already exists because we are human; so, we do not need to think about how it can have come into existence in the first place.

The enigma of society is that after three thousand years of written scholarship we still go to war and dump poison in the sea. But going deeper than that: neither philosophy, economics nor sociology can take the irrational messiness of emotion into account. And yet it triggers so much of our actual social behaviour, rough and ready as it unfortunately is.

When we take a wrong turn, when we lose the plot, when we realise that we're not finding the answers, that's when fantasies, rhetoric, and bullshit flourish. This reminds me of the Oozlum bird. In 2018, Wikipedia reported:

> The Oozlum bird is a legendary creature found in Australian and British folk tales and legends. Some versions have it that, when startled, the bird will take off and fly around in ever-decreasing circles until it manages to fly up itself, disappearing completely, which adds to its rarity. Other sources state that the bird flies backwards so that it can admire its own beautiful tail-feathers or because, while it does not know where it is going, it likes to know where it has been.

I love that bit about disappearing up itself, adding to its rarity. The Oozlum bird consumes itself; not unlike some of the required reading which is handed out to sociology and philosophy students today.

When striving for Seth Abrutyn's sociological paradigm shift, the distinction between assembly and performance could be a good place to start, and Darwin's natural selection could be a useful machete for hacking our way through the tangled thickets of myth, religion and hubris.

Obscure words can make reading difficult. Words like palimpsest and eponymous get picked up and played about with on radio and TV, then after misuse and overexposure in quizzes and intellectual discussions they quietly disappear. Hermeneutics is a good example; it was originally the name given to the study of how to interpret the Christian Bible, but now it is also used to mean interpretation in its more general sense. So, to the innocent reader it's an incomprehensible word which, when you look it up, turns out to be about comprehension. That's a word that vanishes up itself. Neologism is another; it is a newly invented word meaning 'newly invented word'.

Bashing an Idea into Shape

But joking apart, getting somebody's meaning is a serious matter especially in the Western world where, since we nearly all speak derivatives of Latin and Greek, it's deceptively easy to misunderstand each other. The closer we get to a lingua franca the worse it gets. The problem here is comprehension. Words can easily fly up themselves; difficult words in this quick-fire game can escape to fool about in the sky with the Oozlum bird, and if you think you're going to need a dictionary you won't be allowed to join in the fun.

Why-oh-why do scholars have to use obscure words in their learned journals? Well the obvious answer is that everyday words are too vague for them. So, scholars collectively are compelled to invent their own 'shorthand' dictionary of specialised words and phrases to bounce their meanings off each other. They know what they mean. We accountants know what we mean by 'discounted cash flow'. Medievalists doing Chaucer studies actually speak Old English among themselves at their international conferences. Though I am no scholar, I'm guilty of it myself; I often fail to use everyday words.

Let us say I have a terrific idea. It starts in my head like a 3-D cloud; a vague concept, a dream that looks like a ball of wool. It hardly ever arrives as an orderly stream of English words. If I'm to get this idea across to you I'll have to collect the elements into carefully picked words and phrases in a language you happen to use. Then I'll have to combine, order and put them down on a flat sheet of paper. That means in two dimensions; all over the page with arrows and rubbings out, like the blackboard in a physics seminar.

Then the words and symbols on this untidy 2-D sheet must be bashed out into one single stream, one after the other, in the best order I can devise. That's the only way in which you, my listener/reader can then take them in; one word after the other; there is absolutely no alternative. A diagram, picture, flow-chart or graph may short-circuit the process slightly but at the point of contact between us we will still have to use a single, one-dimensional, stream of words.

To comprehend my brilliant idea, you must then hear or read this single stream of words.

Finally, you have to expand them in your head, interpreting as you go, so that the understandings which you form in your head are much the same as I hope them to be. Until you have done that I have failed; at best there has only been partial comprehension.

And it was my fault.

The Oozlum bird has evolved its beautiful tail-feathers to enable it to excel in these comprehension-confusion games. And the natural selection of myths, which ensures that only the most useful survive, explains why the lovely bird thrives despite repeatedly flying up itself.

PART 1

SOCIAL REALITY

Social Reality; Primary Reality

In her delightful monologue 'George Don't Do That', Joyce Grenfell's imaginary little schoolchildren soaked up social reality like blotting paper. From their first few months, human babies are keenly alert. Then at kindergarten, socialising is more or less the only thing they do; often to the despair of teachers trying to interest them in coloured wooden blocks; and later in reading, writing and arithmetic.

Social reality comes in through our senses as we see, hear and remember the significance of what's going on around us. One can think of this as *primary* social reality so as to distinguish it from the *secondary* receipts, opinions, interpretations and explanations which we store away after processing primary data.

Six Imaginary People

PART 1 looks at social reality as it is experienced by six imaginary people: a child, a student, an apprentice, a mother, an employee and finally a senior citizen. In Chaucer's *Canterbury Tales*, each member in a group of pilgrims has a different angle on society and how it works. Via this multi-layered device he gave us a wonderful, warts and all, set of snapshots of fourteenth-century England. In honour of Chaucer, this life-stages approach is adopted in PART 1. This is an alternative to the more usual story which builds chronologically to the present day through the works of famous men; it is simply a different way to review the wonders of our social lives.

What is society all about? How does it work? We wonder about it from childhood to old age, and it's interesting to see how the answers differ as we age. For example, The Mother's Tale uses a down-to-earth distinction between things and non-things to cut through the epistemology, ontology and hermeneutics spouted by her university-student daughter. So far as the mother is concerned, if it looks like a duck, walks like a duck and quacks like a duck, then it is a duck.

Social reality is more confined than philosophy. Its debating points are mainly restricted to the questions we find playing around on the borderline between individual and member of a group. The question, 'Who am I?' sometimes conflicts with, 'Who are we?' Many of these questions are left dangling in PART 1. They are presented as unsolved puzzles, parcelled up so that they can be revisited for possible solution in PART 3 Illuminations, where answers are suggested.

A question which crops up several times in PART 1, is whether it is more realistic to think of society as a collection of individual people, or as being made up of inter-related hierarchies of groups.

Individual people can be collected into statistics and used as the raw material of economic theory. This material includes numbers of motorists, demographic population studies, power consumption, the supply of and demand for goods and services, numbers employed in specific industries, numbers out of work, borrowings per head, GDP, and so on. These 'macro' numbers may be easy to manipulate and predict, they may be good for marketing and for feeding the newspapers, but statistics don't seem to tell the real story of daily life as we apprentices, mothers and senior citizens live it. They tell little or nothing about the quality or the spirit of our existence. Most of what goes on in life, most of what is actually done, is done by working groups; not by individuals acting alone. Groups seem to be more realistic components for the study of society than individuals.

By 'groups' I mean individuals first assembled and then performing in working units; units in which labour is divided to get the benefits of cooperation. We are all keenly aware that the life we live is an inter-networking rough and tumble of families, local communities, criminal gangs, work-places, shops, charities, sports clubs, online cyber-groups, doctor's surgeries, tax-men, solicitors, business corporations and nations; these are the real features of our everyday lives. They inhabit the pond we swim in. Each one is essentially ambitious and self-serving; each is a unit with its own identity and boundaries. The problem, which is examined repeatedly here in PART 1, is that it's more or less impossible to make sense of the bewildering array of group interactions within this set-up. It obviously works; the human is an extremely successful animal, but how does it function? Who is in charge? That's not an easy question. Social Network Analysis is a brilliant way of displaying these interactions in chart form, but that is all it can do; it cannot explain the dynamics in play.

Assembly and performance thinking will be offered in PART 2 as an idea which might help us to understand it all. This way of thinking may be novel but it's quite simple to grasp; it does not require any statistics or mathematics and is much less complicated than classical economic theory. It is not going to be the usual set of ideas about how to put right the failings, unfairness or breakdowns of society; it is a Darwinian quest into how society actually does work. It is an explanation of dynamic workings not a description of statics or a 'naming of parts'. It is a set of ideas which is welded together by the doctrine of natural selection, so PART 2 will be coldly devoid of questions about how society ought to work.

My best excuse here against accusations of callous inhumanity is that it is better to try to understand the Devil than to pretend he isn't there at all.

THE CHILD'S TALE

Primary Reality Comes through the Senses

I was once a new-born, we all were; totally innocent, eyes gradually lighting up, we looked around. Reality came rushing in through our eyes, ears, fingers and stomachs, and it was registered, manipulated and remembered.

'Where am I, which way is up, what is real, what's happening?'

'Yes indeed, my dear little thing, you may well ask. What is real?'

Our senses are somehow more primitive, more compelling, than our reason. Pain beats argument. The primacy of the 'things' we perceive with our senses over the 'non-things' of our reason is confirmed by the order in which an infant gets to know the world. From day one we start to make sense of the reality of concrete, tangible things. Sounds we have already heard in the womb are now connected up with what we can see. Nutrient digestion reveals it's ugly function.

By the age of two, curious children have always wondered: 'Mummy, if I shut my eyes and block my ears and everything vanishes, does that mean things are only there when my eyes are open?' In my day mothers would answer, 'You'll have to ask your father.'

At around three, when we have started talking, remembering and asking questions, we become aware of death. We are then fed the classic nursery-rhyme answers, ready-made in folklore and religion. That's the stage at which reasoning begins; the point here is that reasoning comes after, and depends on, the registration and recording of primary or sensory reality.

The father might remember that in Western philosophy there are two great schools of thought. One is *rationalism*, which says that ultimate reality can only be proved to exist by the power of thought. Frenchman René Descartes, with his 'Cogito ergo sum' or 'I know I'm real', was the top rationalism man; he thought it all out. The opposing school, *empiricism*, says that ultimate reality can only come to us through our five senses: sight, sound, touch, taste and smell. The big man here was David Hume, the renowned Scottish sceptic.

The father could add that in one form or another, this philosophical dichotomy – 'What's dichotomy Mummy?' – has reverberated throughout the centuries, that it reappears constantly in the philosophical textbooks, and that the thoughtful child will often meet it again. At this point the little sister is counting her toes, already convinced that nothing is real unless she can chew it.

Politics

Socialising at home is then gradually enriched by the Joyce Grenfell effect. This final stage in a toddler's social education is the big one. It's about the cynical politics of group behaviour. The child soaks up rules of behaviour from its family and from playing around with its peers. Who is the boss? Why are some things naughty and not others?

The child comes to suspect that the so-called truths, realities and rules it has been taught incessantly since the year dot, are not always to be trusted. As the song goes in the Rogers and Hammerstein 1949 musical, *South Pacific*: 'You've got to be taught from year to year . . . to hate all the people your relatives hate.'

Those parental truths and realities may be internally consistent and publicly endorsed, but the thinking child senses that if they all depend on the same notion of a higher realm of ideal principles, in other words on God, these 'truths' could well be false. This is when rebellion can set in.

Like my sisters and brother, and like children all over the world, I soaked up this knowhow. Questions buzzed endlessly: Why are some things disgraceful and not others? Who is the real boss? Why are lies sometimes OK and how is it best to tell them? The answers we'd been given since the dawn of our understanding were based on kings, princesses, heroes, magicians, warriors and monsters, on God and the devil. And of course, things like sex were completely unmentionable. Well in Protestant Dublin they were. Even Roman Catholics were sort of 'other' (I've chosen that word carefully here).

We didn't take long to realise that these answers couldn't always be trusted. For example, when I was at school we had to pray for 'Jews, Turks and Infidels' which seemed rather arrogant. If all the answers relied on God, and if God had to be a matter of belief, and if my father himself didn't actually seem to believe in God, then all these answers could well be false.

When mucking about with schoolfriends, meeting Roman Catholics and foreigners who had difficulty speaking English, these standard answers got tested even further. Mistakes could get you into trouble. Trusting strangers could be a dangerous game.

Political lessons come in stages; the infant notices that family life follows cyclical daily moods. From morning to night, the recurring patterns of life are punctuated and pushed along by helping, trust, shouting, punishment, rules and obedience. I learnt that hunger, fear and sex did not motivate only me; they affected the whole family. My elder sister was terrific at pushing politely at the boundaries, and this occasionally activated the whole family *as a cooperating unit*; one had to keep up with which boyfriend was in favour at any one time and one was usually sworn to secrecy about it.

Naughty or Good

The flexibility of moral judgement was an exciting social puzzle. It became obvious that sex and money can influence the rules. Stealing sweets, flattery, tax-dodging, fare-dodging and minor betrayals were sometimes condoned: 'everybody does it'. But they *are* wrong, so the thinking ten-year-old quickly develops a suspicion that the whole morality-edifice must be riddled with holes. It's a short step from there to wondering whether God, the foundation-stone of it all, actually exists. A male, white-bearded God in heaven, revered by kings and princesses? Really?

The God of the Cosmos

Maybe God-in-heaven is going a bit too far, but when I was ten it seemed obvious, if you go back and back like opening a set of Russian dolls, that time, space and matter must have started. They must, once upon a time, have come into being. And who is to say that God is not concealed in there behind the answers? In 1993, the great physicist Stephen Hawking (*Black Holes and Baby Universes and Other Essays*) famously remarked about the universe that 'If we find the answer to that, it would be the ultimate triumph of human reason – for then we would know the face of God.'

More Questions than Answers

So how are we to define God? There are always more questions than answers, especially to the teenager, but in this book which is about how human society works, it is probably safe to parcel up the deeper ones and put them on the 'Maybe Later' pile.

These bewilderingly recurring patterns of group behaviour, the mechanisms of cooperation, are the subject of this book. They are naturally selected, by the will to survive and prosper. And we cannot survive as solitaries outside our groups.

When we were children, we were promised that there was nothing to worry about because these regularities have all been fully explained by the great thinkers of history, and that one day we would understand them.

In fact, of course, we still have little idea of how human society really works. Why do we go to war? Why can't we prevent corporate greed? Why do we go on pumping smoke into the air and dumping plastic into the sea? Do the same social mechanisms organise the behaviour of every team, orchestra, church, business corporation, army brigade and criminal gang? Might these mechanisms be similar to those at work in other social animals; even in social microbes?

Though our biologists believe they can explain the advanced social behaviour of the Portuguese man o' war, leaf-cutter ant and killer whale, we seem strangely inhibited from taking a similarly objective view of human society. Cooperation occurs throughout nature and yet we routinely overlook the mechanisms humans use to achieve it.

41

Without cooperation society is impossible and without society a person would quickly perish, but for some reason the regularities of the human cooperating group seen as a unit are usually ignored – taken for granted. Why? Why is it that Western philosophy, though it has volumes to say about society, focuses primarily on how the individual human should live its social life but says more or less nothing on the nature of the group as an item; the group as a thing in its own right? Why do we routinely ignore the underlying mechanisms of cooperation?

These are some of the questions I am going to try to answer in PART 2.

That ends The Child's Tale. Next, let's look at social reality from a student's angle.

> Close as he dared he drew himself to look
> And listened carefully to work and part
> Until he knew the opening verse by heart.
> He had no notion what this Latin meant
> Being so young, so tender too, so green;
> But in the end, one morning there, he went
> And asked a comrade what the song might mean
> And why it was in use. He was so keen
> To know it that he went down upon his knees
> Begging the boy to explain it if he please.

From *The Prioress's Tale*, Geoffrey Chaucer

THE STUDENT'S TALE

Social Reality Comes in through Teaching and on the Merry-go-Round of Life

When we were students the world was at our feet. In 1949, when I went to university, the Second World War was just over. We were adult, away from home, and lively. Our generation was extrovert, optimistic, idealistic, privileged, sporting, humanist, left wing . . . OK, yes to all that, but the reality seemed a bit more complicated. It was a daunting matter of stepping out on to the world stage.

Had I been born a German might I have been an enthusiastic member of the Hitler Youth? Of course not, I told myself, but I was the right age, having been born in 1931, and from 1939 to 1945 I was quite unsure about who I was; Anglo-Irish yes, but otherwise thoroughly mixed up. Lucky escape there.

We were competitive, we had learned about that at school. But we were also confused and rebellious, and of course many of us, though interested, were quite hopeless with girls. Several of them were beautiful.

Away from home for the first time the girl or boy soaks up the sudden freedom, trying to make sense of life. Religion comes knocking, so do philosophy and poetry. These all help with the difficult business of sorting things out, and so does sport.

The typical student is not very bothered about making a way in the world, at least not yet; there are other things to be sorted out first. Like: Who am I? How do I look in a crowd? What's my level in the pecking order? Am I personally attractive? . . . Popular? . . . Who do I admire?

And then there are the social options: clubs to join, skills to polish, new friendships. There are drinking sessions, and naughtiness. Drugs and love mix hypnotically, it's a dangerous and exciting whirlwind full of fantasies and dreams, with the occasional wild prank to push the boundaries.

Everything is possible but firmly within the bounds of social reality. And there it is again, social reality, the great deflator of dreams.

Rowing and Sex

While studying Economics and Political Science at Trinity College Dublin (TCD) in the early 1950s, I took up rowing. After two years in maiden and junior crews I was immensely proud to be selected to row at bow in the university senior eight which went over to England to compete at Henley Regatta in 1952.

The thing about rowing is that it requires unison. A crew of fit young women who move precisely together will easily beat a much stronger but uncoordinated crew of equally fit young men. There seems to be something deep in our animal nature which imparts joy to crew members when working together in perfect unison. I guess it must be to do with being a co-operator; being an animal which has evolved the responses necessary for participation in labour-divided groups. No group; no survival.

It is said that singing in a choir and playing in an orchestra give similarly transcendent feelings of being almost one body. Team games like football and cricket trigger the joy of cooperation too, of course, and so does dancing, but less intensely than rowing. That's because for good rowing you must be able to keep moving in precise coordination with your team-mates and keep that up for several miles; sometimes even when exhausted to the point of collapse. Most races are won in training. By the day of the actual race the best trained crew usually wins.

The intensity of the pleasure available from good rowing can probably be explained by the way it touches our 'cooperation nerve'; it encourages us to do one of the most essential things in life – to cooperate effectively. It reminds me of a scene in Peter Shaffer's play, *Equus*, when the horse gets pleasure from being groomed; a pleasure transmitted to the groom which encourages her to work effectively, the better to remove harmful little creatures. Natural selection favours responses that are useful for survival, in horses and meerkats as well as humans.

Good rowing can be more satisfying than sex; books on rowing often acknowledge this but rowers seldom do. I think that's because crew relations are so intense that sex talk violates each other's privacy. It's interesting that successful crews have often included members who heartily disliked each other. Mutual trust is not quite the same thing as friendship. Personal differences are suspended in successful teamwork. Big lesson there in reality, and social reality is the subject of PART 2.

Anyway, as Philip Larkin famously said in his poem *Annus Mirabilis*, sex was not invented till 1963, and that was in England. In Ireland it came later. In the early 1950s at TCD I learnt more from rowing about how society actually works than I did from any lectures, and of course that's the stamp of a great university; and TCD was one of the best.

The Good News about Jobs

Once they had graduated, the students then had to make their way in the world. Some, newly qualified in medicine or civil engineering, had little difficulty getting started. For others it was not always so easy. Today, every July and August, the newspapers print stories spiced with unemployment statistics, about how robotics and computerised information technology are destroying manual and managerial jobs. My neighbour Anna Wilson, no relation, gave a course of lectures on Creative Writing at Bath Spa University. A student, she says, can get anxious about this bleak outlook; the work she would have done ten years ago has now been automated; will she ever find a job when she graduates? Just as she sets out on life, the 'social pyramid' – wage slaves and temporary workers at the bottom, bosses at the top – seems to be getting ever smaller and steeper.

All this statistically fuelled gloom comes from the *homo economicus* angle, where the self-motivated individual is the basis of society. But the social individual, referred to here as *homo reciprocans*, is a bit different. (For more on these two angles see People Studies below.) As well as being self-motivated, *homo reciprocans* is altruistic. So how does this angle affect the prospects of a student setting out to make a living?

It may help here to go back to basics again so here goes: The essential things an animal does in life can always be boiled down to three functions: *metabolism [M]*, which is the energy-acquisition system of eating and so on, *self-protection [S-P]*, which is the adaptation to surroundings, and *breeding [B]*.

Humans, I cannot say it often enough, are intensely cooperative creatures. Almost everything we do in life; we do in groups. Each group is a separate self-motivated social unit in its own right and within each of these units the cooperative division of labour makes performance marvellously efficient. These groups include families, criminal gangs, charities, clubs, businesses, armies, factories, hospitals, shops, farms, terrorist groups, transport systems, and more. The work each group does always performs one or more of these three (M, S-P and B) functions. And while performing these functions they bash themselves into a more or less harmonious hierarchy; a hierarchy which *emerges* naturally; it settles itself into the overall pattern we call society.

This is the *homo reciprocans* angle. It seems more realistic for the youngster to think of herself as about to join one of these knockabout groups rather than as a statistic 'entering the job market'. Admittedly the standard economic person, *homo economicus*, with her standard wants and needs, can be added up, compared, graphed over time, correlated mathematically to events and other statistics; she can be fed into statistical models, the playthings of professors and PhDs; she can be ground out in statistics and economics which stretch way out over the horizon. But the standard person can't be used to construct what goes on in everyday labour-divided teams all over the world. People often do altruistic things but the statistician's *homo economicus* never does.

One can think of the unemployment confronting the student on graduation as being like a highland pool fed by a stream. The pool keeps a more or less constant level, but the individual students swirling through are changing all the time, so there's no need to worry; she'll be swept in, swirled about a bit and poured out the other side. Unemployment statistics don't recognise the individuals: only the water level.

So, the message from *homo reciprocans* is: 'You're not a statistic you're an individual and one way or another you're wanted in the great engine of society; it needs you. It's up to you to choose where you would like to fit in. Be patient, even in the toughest times there are always jobs around. You should join the best team that will accept you and go from there. If you don't have good qualifications it may have to be a menial job but once you've started, you're in.'

This isn't to deny the great usefulness of statistics, but they do need to be kept firmly under control, otherwise it's easy to lose sight of social reality. Easy, for example, to believe that motorists are units of traffic, 'them', when actually they are you and me; 'us'. Truthful statistics support valuable policies by adding together, comparing and manipulating data from across wide fields. But they are easily sensationalised on TV and radio in the competition for biggest circulation. The result is that it's easy to lose sight of reality; easy to live in a media-created, hyped-up imaginary world in which pressure-groups drown out the silent majority. Social reality concerns family, team and tribe. The point here is not the old one about 'lies, damn lies and statistics', it is that statistics frequently loosen our grip on social reality.

Religion

Theology should have been able to clarify the realities of this rich new life, and for some students it did. Religion claims to have a lot of the answers about death, how to behave in society, and so on. As a Christian teenager I had earnestly wanted to be a believer, and I went through the Christian 'confirmation' ceremony but all that body of Christ stuff, the miracles, and God enthroned on high, were a bit much. I could almost have accepted their beliefs, but when, in answer to my sharpest test-question, they denied that Joey, my beloved bull terrier, had a soul my faith evaporated.

I had been brought up a Protestant, not a Roman Catholic, Jew or Muslim, and I saw no reason to deny it. But I couldn't go along with all those crazy beliefs and dogmas. The church seemed to have left me, not me it. When I turned my back on God it left me with a lingering doubt. Who or what is God? If there isn't a God, then what else was the ultimate creator? And surely all that morality stuff spouted from the pulpit about how to behave, God's Ten Commandments and all that, surely that part must have been right?

Atheism did not seem to be the answer. It seemed to be simply the denial of belief, with nothing to put in its place. It was a negative: a negative *waiting for the answers* about the origin of the cosmos. The thoughtful student realises that if these questions are eventually solved one day, then the atheist's solution will itself be a belief. So, by definition, atheism cannot be a good answer; it is a belief system which denies the possibility of belief. So, it's a paradox.

Religion did not offer a realistic explanation of how actually society works. And yet, maybe I'm irrational here, but I have never been able to drop the capital letter in God. Neither in their hearts did Bertrand Russell or Wittgenstein. I think it's out of an innate respect for society.

Party Politics

When I was a student the idea of democracy made perfect sense. We should be governed by the will of the people, not by aristocrats, rich men or bullies. And that was that: one man one vote; simple. So, it was a big let-down to discover that, to be elected, one first had to join a party and that every party had its own policies, policies which were not necessarily one's own. This immediately messed up the sensible idea of the simple majority vote. To a student with things to say it didn't seem quite right. And there was plenty to say. For example, minorities: servants, black people, homosexually-oriented people, these were all around us; we were among them, but in Dublin in the 1950s they had little or no voice in politics. They were ignored, brushed aside. And I'm ashamed to remember that I and my new friends, girls as well as boys, were too selfishly focused on succeeding in the rough and tumble of student life to take much notice of these minorities. Natural selfishness is a powerful motivator, and party politics was an early social-reality lesson about groups having minds of their own which ruthlessly boss us individuals about.

People Studies: Homo Economicus versus Homo Reciprocans

Economics and Political Science was an interesting degree course on offer in the early 1950s. It was designed to prepare a youngster for a useful life in society, so that was the one I chose. But the Second World War was just over, and this field of study was undergoing considerable change; it was confused by powerful undercurrents of social reconstruction. Many social attitudes which had been plain and simple, black and white, during the war years, grew alarmingly in complexity.

It was daunting, but we had been taught at school that when daunted it is a good idea to track right back to basic assumptions. Assumption-testing had become a mental habit. One of these was about the proper unit for people studies. Economics and politics are people studies, but in those days the assumptions they relied on were never properly confronted in our lectures or exams. They were not even considered. Economists and statisticians always took it for granted that when building and measuring government policies the individual is the only proper unit of construction to be used. Individuals, they said, must first be counted and sorted before they can be built up into measures of performance such as gross domestic product – GDP. This unit of construction, identified by Adam Smith, can be called *homo economicus*.

In quite separate lectures we were told that many sociologists, the intellectual descendants of J. J. Rousseau, recognised that in real life, society is made up of labour-divided indivisible units like tribes, principalities and nations, whose behaviour cannot be boiled down to the sum of their individual members. These are units, Rousseau and others said, whose collective will cannot be discerned by simple majority vote. These theorists take the group rather than the individual as the proper unit of study. In tribute to Pyotr Kropotkin, who introduced the expression, this unit of theory-construction is referred to here as *homo reciprocans*.

Economic individual or group; *homo economicus* or *homo reciprocans*? It's not until recently that I have come to understand that this was a big unsolved social-reality question when I was a student. There is still no definitive answer today.

In his comprehensive textbook *The Emergence of Social Theory* (2001), J. H. Robb traces the history of social theory from ancient times to the present day. Throughout his review runs the question: 'What's the proper unit for study?' His final statement on page 272 reads as follows:

> Among the old debates which reappeared in new forms and contexts, perhaps the most fundamental for the social sciences was that of the relationship between the concepts of individuals and groups . . . A consideration of the history of these fluctuations of view through the centuries suggests the possibility that theories emphasising the importance of individuals and the unreality of groups may tend to arise among the wealthier and powerful classes and become more widely accepted in times of affluence, while times of stress, poverty and lack of hope are more conducive to the spread of beliefs in the importance and reality of groups, and of the need for a strengthening of the bonds of community.

It is a nice idea, but I'm not entirely convinced. The alternative notion offered here is that we need to start with the prior, and more basic, question of how it is that individuals, inherently selfish, can actually manage to assemble into groups in the first place. Assembly and performance thinking are the subject of PART 2 below.

Nevertheless, I respectfully acknowledge J. H. Robb's scholarship. It helped me to understand how social theory developed over the years. His distinction between economists and social theorists would have been invaluable in my student days. Throughout his *The Emergence of Social Theory*, and almost as a side issue, Robb delicately sorted the main schools of sociology into economists in the tradition of Adam Smith or group thinkers in the tradition of J. J. Rousseau. But sadly, I didn't notice its significance until fifty-five years later. I will be using the terms *homo economicus* and *homo reciprocans* to mark the distinction.

The Feudal System: Individual or Group?

It's all very well telling a student, 'The world is your oyster' but what world? Where is it? What's it like? Is the archbishop in charge or is it the king? There are so many different versions. What versions did the Ancient Egyptians use, or the Irish in feudal times?

Modern European society emerged gradually out of the medieval era. Today we tend to dismiss medieval life as having been dark and brutish, but it was underpinned by the feudal system. This was a recognisable set of social structures and beliefs which were robust enough to last about eight hundred years, from the breakdown of the Roman civilisation in AD600 to the Renaissance. Whatever we may think of it, the feudal system worked as long as did the rule of Roman law. That's a social reality which can't be dismissed as an aberration.

Here's what J. H. Robb says about the feudal system:

> This system was a form of social organisation based on the idea of a ruler who 'owned' his territory, which he had acquired by inheritance or conquest. His personal followers were given control over substantial fractions of his territory in return for

pledges of loyalty and guarantees of armed support in his wars. The followers subdivided their territories and obligations in the same way and so on down through the system to the lowest rank (the serfs) who were little more than chattels tied to the land which they worked in exchange for a bare living and the promise of protection by the forces of their lord. Thus there was a close intertwining of the economy (essentially rural in nature), a political system based on armed force (especially the use of heavily armed cavalry), their associated technologies, and an aristocratic social system (whose upper-class males provided the manpower for the cavalry). Fitted together with all these was an elaborate culture and ideology of chivalry, courtly love and troubadours.

So, feudal society very clearly saw itself from the viewpoint of *homo reciprocans* rather than *economicus*. Society was understood to be composed of nested hierarchies of labour-divided cooperating units: villages, baronies, principalities and kingdoms; not, as in the Roman system, of individuals which could be counted, manipulated and measured, and ruled by Roman law. The feudal system understood groups more clearly than it understood individuals.

In his scholarly book *Chaucer and the Subject of History*, Lee Patterson points out that one must 'think socially' to get the proper context of Geoffrey Chaucer's wonderful poetry.

... however much Chaucer may have been absorbed into the ideology of individualism that has come to dominate Anglo-American thinking, and however much his poetry may have solicited such co-option, he also thought, and imagined, socially.

There's a striking contrast between the feudal system and late Victorian England. Basil Chubb, our professor of sociology at TCD, kept reminding us of the words of Walter Bagehot, proud describer of the British Empire: 'The state is an association which, acting through law as promulgated by a government, endowed to this end with a coercive power, maintains within a community, territorially demarcated, the universal, external conditions of order.' No recognition of distinct self-motivated businesses or social units there; Bagehot's nation state is presented like a butcher's carcass for analysis by the school of *homo economicus*. It is an item to be modelled with the powerful mathematical tools of economics and statistics.

Winston Churchill once said that though democracy doesn't work very well, it's the best we've got. But it's useful to remember that democracy is by no means the only alternative. European feudalism was one of many possible social structures that have worked well for long stretches of time. Today we seem to be groping, worldwide, for the best structure to suit the electronic age and Churchill's version of democracy may not be the winner. The most successful future social model, be it Scandinavian, Japanese, Latin American, Syrian, Congolese, Cuban or whatever, is likely to be established by the weeding-out process of the natural selection of political systems.

The natural selection of the fittest among competing social structures was promoted by Herbert Spencer as we shall shortly come to see below.

Economics and Political Science at TCD

As students of economics and political science in the early 1950s, we sat exams about the great men who had helped to develop modern European social structures from those medieval times. This was the age of the Industrial Revolution, described by R. H. Tawney in his *Religion and the Rise of Capitalism*, as an age when religion was giving way to capitalism.

The honours degree in Economics and Political Science at TCD required a deep immersion in classical economics: Adam Smith, Ricardo, *homo economicus* and all that stuff. Looking back now I realise that my inability to accept, let alone understand, their books must have been due to childhood. Struggling as an eight-year-old to understand what was going on I had become instinctively biased towards the group as the best approach. So later I intuitively favoured the school of *homo reciprocans*. Maybe that is self-justification but it's my excuse for only just scraping through with a pass.

Here are a few of the great men distinguishing *homo reciprocans* from *homo economicus*.

Thomas Hobbes (1588–1679)

Thomas Hobbes was one of the earliest and most penetrating social commentators; the earliest in any field are often the best. He published *Leviathan* in 1651 in which he depicted what we now call 'the corporation' as the great sea monster of the Christian Old Testament. His subtitle, *The Matter, Form and Power of a Commonwealth, Ecclesiastical and Civil*, suggests that as well as to the church and the state, his ideas were also relevant to the trade guilds, leagues, and other multinational corporations; mercenary standing armies for example, which existed in his day.

Hobbes recognised that on our own, without society, we humans would be powerless, and that life would be 'solitary, poor, nasty, brutish and short'. I would emphasise the *solitary* here. This, he said, gave rise to the social contract: 'and reason suggesteth convenient articles of peace, upon which men may be drawn by agreement'. In this contract, power and liberty are surrendered to the chief executive in exchange for law and order. When we equate Hobbes's leviathan with the giant multi-national corporation of the twenty-first century, his view is still a hundred per cent relevant today.

If Hobbes had delved deeper below the level of the nation-state, he would have been on the threshold of describing society as a nested hierarchy of labour-divided cooperating units.

The competing corporations and conglomerates of today, the giant multinationals, are essentially independent. Some even dwarf the states they operate in. They are uncannily like Hobbes's collection of independently competing leviathans; the principalities, republics like Venice, ruthless great trading houses, the Condottieri, the religious orders and the Hanseatic League. But Hobbes failed to notice what Chaucer and others had recognised all along: that every society has always consisted of small groups within the giants, and still smaller discrete teams operating within those small groups, each with its own ambitions, external boundaries and internal mechanisms. Nevertheless,

I claim Hobbes as one of the earliest *Homo reciprocans* sociologists; he didn't do statistics.

Jean-Jacques Rousseau (1712–1778)

J. H. Robb describes Rousseau's motivations as follows:

> His emphasis changed from reason to emotion. Similarly his philosophical theory shows a movement from individualism to collectivism in the sense that he became concerned with society, not so much as a summation of individuals (the will of all), but rather as an organic unity, the expression of what he called the 'general will'.

Rousseau applied this insight in several radical debates. For example, it was he who made the famous statement: 'Man is born free and everywhere he is in chains.' His concept of a 'general will' has reverberated down the centuries. It was an important insight and it clearly places Rousseau as the most influential Western sociologist since Jesus Christ to re-establish the *homo reciprocans* camp. But it was to be many years before anyone took the next step. This was to recognise that 'the general will' idea applies not just to the nation-state but to every labour-divided social group within its nested hierarchy. This did not truly happen until the twentieth century when the rise of business schools turned the spotlight on to this particular type of cooperating unit.

Bernard Mandeville (1670–1733)

A few decades before Rousseau, Bernard Mandeville had written *The Fable of the Bees* (1714) in which he suggested that, by natural evolutionary processes, unruly individuals develop the habit of subordinating their selfish desires to the general welfare. This was well published in England at the time but quickly faded from view. That's a shame because Mandeville deftly put his finger on the essence of what I call assembly and performance thinking. He related human society to honey-bee society, indicating our animal nature. He also recognised that the group, having a mind of its own, is a self-motivated unit. It has taken at least two hundred years to listen to what he said. We can all be very stupid at times. Mandeville, also a *homo reciprocans*, was essentially a cheerful optimist, whereas Rousseau was a bad-tempered pessimist whose strident ideas fuelled the French Revolution.

Adam Smith (1723–1790)

Adam Smith is widely recognised as the father of modern economics.

To quote J. H. Robb:

> More than any previous writer Smith moved from broad philosophical generalisations about science and scientific method as applied to social phenomena to firm statements about the ways in which cause and effect operated in economic activities.

Robb goes on to say:

> Smith, like Locke, Hume and their continental contemporaries, with the partial exception of Rousseau, accepted that the proper unit for the study of society was the individual and his psychological processes.

Adam Smith, admiring Isaac Newton's achievements in understanding the cosmos, wanted to develop a similarly scientific self-regulating system of the workings of human society. His ideas greatly influenced the thinking of the Industrial Revolution. Smith was the original *homo economicus*.

Laissez-Faire

The policy of minimum government interference in taxation, trade tariffs, interest rates and the other levers of economic performance has surfaced regularly since the eighteenth century.

Here's what Wikipedia said in April 2018 about laissez-faire:

1. The individual is the basic unit in society.

2. The individual has a natural right to freedom.

3. The physical order of nature is a harmonious and self-regulating system.

4. Corporations are the creatures of the State and therefore must be watched closely by the citizenry due to their propensity to disrupt the [Adam] Smithsonian spontaneous order.

....

Laissez-faire is ultimately a selfish policy favouring one's own group, tribe, corporation or nation. It's obvious that if everybody fully follows this policy then everybody eventually suffers from mutual retaliation. Unfortunately, the doctrine contains no logical halfway house or point of equilibrium. This was Margaret Thatcher's downfall and, if he's not careful, it could well see the end of Donald Trump too.

Despite popping up again and again in politics, laissez-faire regularly ends up making a mess of things. A particularly notorious example was the nineteenth-century Irish Potato Famine whose devastating effects reverberated for well over a century. A policy of laissez-faire prevented the British government from stepping in with the plainly obvious reliefs that could have saved millions of lives. This blunder was repeated continuously between 1845 and 1849. As John Mitchel, a leader of the Young Ireland Movement, wrote in 1860: 'The almighty, indeed, sent the potato blight, but the English created the famine.'

Laissez-faire lurks below the surface of social theory. It is what happens when *homo economicus* gets out of control and falls into in the hands of inept demagogues.

David Ricardo (1772–1823)

In conjunction with James Mill, father of John Stuart Mill, David Ricardo studied political economy. In his own words he defined this as 'the laws which determine the division of the produce of industry among the classes which concur in its formulation.' Ricardo took no interest in the nature of the labour-divided group. He failed to see it as a distinct and significant creature with a mind of its own powerfully prowling the economic jungle. Ricardo was firmly in the camp of *homo economicus*. In J. H. Robb's words: 'The belief in Political Economy as a strictly scientific discipline based on discoverable and reliable laws was one of Ricardo's major, lasting influences on economic thought. Whether this influence was for good or ill has been much debated.'

Henri Saint-Simon (1760–1825)

Saint-Simon, a minor aristocrat who narrowly escaped the guillotine during the French Revolution, was another scholar who strived to establish a complete science of mankind. He too searched for a gravity-equivalent to do for sociology what Newton had done for cosmology. His belief that physiological groupings or classes of society, such as scientists, artists, businessmen and manual workers, should be an important element in any solution, led him to recognise the importance of the group in social studies. To quote J. H. Robb once again:

Saint-Simon believed strongly in the perfectibility of humanity, but he saw this not as most of the philosophes prior to Rousseau had seen it, as a process of perfecting individuals and hence perfecting the society which they had designed for themselves, but as a process for perfecting the society and hence the individuals who lived in it. This contrast between the emphasis on the individual and emphasis on the group

> constituted an important and complex theme in the history
> of this period and has continued in various forms to the
> present day.

So, Robb recognises Saint-Simon as an early exponent of *homo recipricans*. I will claim in PART 2 that sociology can blossom if it distinguishes between the mechanisms of group assembly and those of group performance, and I suggest that the *homo economicus* camp cannot intelligently do this.

Auguste Comte (1798–1857)

Comte, one of Saint-Simon's secretaries, was undoubtedly one of the founders of modern sociology. It was he who invented the very word 'sociology' to distinguish the search for scientific principles from a branch of statistics. Many of Comte's ideas, which were vigorously promoted in England by J. S. Mill, came from his teacher Saint-Simon. Notably they both based their search for scientific principles on the idea that human society always goes through three stages of intellectual development: theological, metaphysical and scientific. These stages, Comte said, occur repeatedly in all branches of knowledge.

Comte unfortunately did not develop Saint-Simon's perception of distinct social groups, so sadly this father of modern sociology cannot be claimed as a *homo reciprocans* man.

Karl Marx (1818–1883)

Back in the late 1940s when I was a student, the cold war with Russia had just begun. Most of Europe had been shattered by World War II,

Ireland was impoverished. Communism was a dirty word and Marxism reminded us of the miseries of the French Revolution. Even socialism was dangerous. But now, in the early twenty-first century, Karl Marx is ranked alongside Durkheim and Weber as one of the three giants of modern sociology. Things change.

Marx started out as a journalist before he undertook a decades-long study of economics. Georg Hegel had observed that human societies proceed dialectically by oscillating between opposing tendencies. This idea led Marx to develop his main thesis: that Western nations would inevitably swing from the phase of laissez-faire capitalism into the age of socialism. With Friedrich Engels, he wrote a manifesto for Communism. This amounted to an assault on capitalism, which to the mainstream intellectual elite seemed erratic.

In my days at TCD this was a conversation of the deaf. For as J. H. Robb put it: 'With economists ostentatiously disassociating themselves from anything that smacked of sociology (or any other branch of social science) there was a decreasing temptation for sociologists to concern themselves with even main-line economics.'

But after Marx died in 1883 the ominously growing miseries of the industrial work-force, the proletariat, had started to make people pay attention to what he had said, and it was a short step from there to the emergence of the socialist movement which in 1917 led to Russian-style Communism. Mainstream intellectuals soon knew themselves to have been swept up in exactly the dialectical process that Marx had predicted, and his posthumous reputation grew and grew.

The economists of the eighteenth and nineteenth centuries: Smith, Ricardo, Marshal and others, had dealt with the individual, with *homo economicus*, as the starting point for their theories. This meant that they were not intellectually equipped to deal with the upheavals and miseries of the Industrial Revolution. As a result, they were brushed aside by those whose ideas were based instead on the labour-divided group, on *homo reciprocans*, as the proper building block. And it was Marx who got the pendulum swinging the other way.

A good way to understand Karl Marx, and the phenomenon of Marxism, which are not the same thing, is to try and label him as either a statistical or social sociologist. It seems clear that Marx started in the *homo economics* camp as a journalist coming from a well-to-do family. But then as an economist he was shocked by the way in which economics seemed indifferent to the poverty and oppression of ordinary people, the proletariat. He recognised these as the direct result of unrestrained capitalism, and with Engels he developed the arguments which were to inspire the international Socialist movement. This classifies Marx as *homo reciprocans*; indeed, as one of the greatest. His extensive study of economics enabled him to mount an effective assault on laissez-faire capitalism. His ideas support those scholars of today who see the labour-divided cooperating group, *homo reciprocans*, as the indivisible unit of society.

According to the thinking being promoted here, Karl Marx's analysis of the mechanisms of society, though hugely influential worldwide, was biologically erratic and therefore fundamentally flawed. This is mainly because in his day few people had yet noticed the way in which natural selection has enabled selfish individuals to *assemble* into cooperating groups, and then how it has enabled these groups to perform their purposes.

Herbert Spencer (1820–1903)

Spencer was an English sociologist, a committed disciple of Darwin. He studied the natural selection of human morals and vigorously promoted the idea that cultures compete for dominance. He propagandised the survival of the society with the fittest *culture*. It was he, not Darwin, who coined the phrase 'the survival of the fittest'. He further argued that the reason why there aren't several different species of modern human is because *Homo sapiens* responds to environmental variations by cultural, rather than bodily, adaptations.

Spencer believed that to boost the moral progress and economic prosperity of mankind, societies that are culturally superior should be left free to compete without restraint on the international stage: one might call this 'eugenics for societies.' In other words, he promoted the unrestrained natural selection of societies to enable the best to rise to the top. In his lifetime these essentially laissez-faire proposals appealed greatly to the vigorous, frontiersman spirit of the USA. But the rest of the intellectual world where laissez-faire had become socially unacceptable was less impressed. The idea was dubbed Social Darwinism and Spencer's fame declined after his death in 1903.

During that bike ride around Ireland with John Gibson my career as an executive in big business had come under attack. I tried and failed to escape the corporate greed accusation. So, on getting home, I started researching famous sociologists including Herbert Spencer to try and find out how cooperation actually does work.

How come we all switch behavioural modes so effortlessly? How could a morally well-behaved, self-motivated, private individual turn instantly into a semi-automatic cog: a selfless team player in a greedy cooperating group, and then, at the drop of a hat, flip back again, in a split-second, into a self-motivated private individual? This question is central in the structure/agency debate which is still alive and kicking today (see below in PART 3).

While reading Spencer, which I found difficult, I must have been daydreaming about this mode-switch. I kept wondering do we really switch our behaviour unconsciously between: a) individual mode and b) group mode? Is that what happens to me in my everyday reality? Or should it be from: a) individual into b) cog-in-a-group and then c) cog-in-a-group into group? I couldn't work it out.

Then I thought one might perhaps get round the problem by re-thinking the nature of the group. This progressed into thoughts which, rather than being about how we are able to switch modes between a) individual, b) cog-in-a-group and c) group, became thoughts about the distinction between the *assembly* of a group and its *performance*.

The point here, something I hadn't noticed before, is that these are totally different mechanisms: assembly being a genetically endowed achievement and performance being a trial-and-error process. Perform-ance is a simple process which is driven by a sort of quasi-mind, or group mentality. And this quasi-mind is brought into being by the very purpose for which the group got itself together in the first place. In other words, assembly uses a genetically enabled consensual agreement between otherwise selfish individuals, while performance is a trial-and-error process. The two are quite different.

It was one of those thoughts in the shower which go click. This distinction then quietly offered several promising ways forward. As they fell into place it became clear that these insights applied in an increasingly wide field; they included religion, the seat of power, law-making, the balance of powers, the interplay between reason and emotion, the structure / agency question and several more. This was an interconnected set of insights; a set which might not to be available, *as a set*, to other social theories. So, I gradually cooked up the Assembly and Performance Thinking (A&PT) which is elaborated in PART 2 below. I owe it to Spencer.

Herbert Spencer did not recognise society as a nested hierarchy of interconnected cooperating groups, but his extensive work on cultural evolution and the survival of the fittest *society* classifies him as a *homo reciprocans*, rather than an *economicus*. Spencer's influence did not last long, which is just as well.

Vilfredo Pareto (1848–1923)

Pareto, born into an aristocratic Italian family, was an economist. He was a skilled mathematician. He specialised in mathematical economics and became professor of economics in Lausanne. He was admired by Mussolini. His international reputation was based on the belief that the methodology of physics could be applied to sociology, and that at the same time, to be properly scientific, economics had to be based on what J. H. Robb referred to as 'a scientific sociology'. Pareto regarded most human behaviour, and particularly group behaviour, as not necessarily illogical, but certainly non-logical. For example, when an individual acting as a member of a team does brave things against his own interest, he is according to Pareto being non-logical. I mention Pareto as a statistical sociologist. He belonged to the venerable tradition of *homo economicus* which considers a statistically standardised, self-seeking individual to be the proper building block for social theory.

Ferdinand Tonnies (1855–1936)

Tonnies, a German, was influenced by Hobbes, Comte and Spencer. He is famous for the observation that social units can be categorised as either family-type or business-type. His names for these two types were elaborated in his 1887 book: *Gemeinschaft und Gesellschaft*.

Here's what J. H. Robb thought about it:

> *Gemeinschaft* (community) is the term Tonnies applied to social relationships, based on spontaneity and informality, which are entered into and maintained for their own sake, for the personal, supportive and intimate situation which they provide. *Gesellschaft* (organisation, association), on the other hand, refers to public, purposive, deliberate relationships entered into in order to achieve some ulterior end, not for its own sake.

This may be a bit vague but as the saying goes: 'We all know what he means.' Our intuitive feeling that a distinction of this sort must be useful is probably fed by the fact that we all have well-developed emotional feelings of loyalty, respect, hatred or disgust about these distinctly different social groups in our lives. Love 'em or hate 'em, they range from family and tribe through club and criminal gang to local council, football team, the office, multinational corporation and nation.

The *Gemeinschaft-Gesellschaft* classification has been much discussed over the years. The point I want to make here is not about it being a useful concept, but simply that it reminds sociologists that there is a spectrum of different types of social unit. This array of units, and the way in which they settle into a hierarchy, seems to offer a satisfactory view of social reality.

Unfortunately, being like a rainbow which has no identifiable interstices, this view of reality does not lend itself to statistical manipulation in economics or mathematical modelling. Ferdinand Tonnies is thus classified as a *homo reciprocans*.

Emile Durkheim (1858–1917)

Durkheim was born in the northeast of France. He was an original thinker with an independent nature. In his sociology he was committed to the objectivity of the scientific method. In his *A Short History of Sociological Thought*, Alan Swingewood says: 'In particular Durkheim sought to distinguish sociology, as the science which studies the objective reality of social facts, from psychology, which he defined as the study of individual consciousness.'

Swingewood goes on to say:

. . . Durkheim identified three groups of social facts:

1. Those related to the morphological structure, such as the volume and density of population, territorial organisation, technology (buildings, machines).

2. Social institutions, such as family, religion, political and economic institutions, involving beliefs and practices (the normative sphere).

3. Currents of opinion, collective representations, involving moral concepts, religious dogmas, political and legal rules.

Durkheim made extensive use of statistical methods in his famous studies of suicide. In his book of that name, first published in 1897, he clearly aspired to be a *homo economicus* in the tradition of Adam Smith. He correlated public records of suicide patterns with population facts, and thus demonstrated how to apply such facts to establish an objective science of sociology.

As to the proper building block for use in studying the mechanisms of society, Emile Durkheim in his *The Division of Labour* (written in 1893), recognised that every social group is a mini-society in its own right, and is integrated into the overall social hierarchy.

In *Classical Sociological Theory* (2002), Craig Calhoun points out:

> In *The Division of Labour*, Durkheim confronted the basic question of what holds modern society together. Using an evolutionary approach, his central thesis in the book was that the increasing division of labour in modern societies was taking the place of the conscience collective – the moral consensus or the collective conscience – that marked traditional societies.

So, Durkheim saw the importance of the labour-divided cooperating group in sociological theory. He died at the age of fifty-nine and it is tantalising to think that if he had lived another twenty years, this great thinker would have bridged the gap between the scientific and the normative schools of sociology; the gap between *homo economicus* and *homo reciprocans*. This is what Max Weber (see below) attempted, and he was only fifty-six when he died.

In public life today we are encouraged by the media to think of ourselves as members of a nation. Unless there is a scandal: murder, corruption, etc., we usually take our everyday groups for granted. These include opportunistic street gangs, charities, families and tribes, sports clubs, ruthless political parties and multinational corporations. The reality of daily life is that these associations coexist in a rough-and-tumble nested hierarchy which makes up a more or less harmonious society.

Durkheim, like Comte before him, strove for a scientifically objective explanation of the workings of society, but this objectivity was quickly swept aside as unkind and heartless by the human-welfare scholarship of Max Weber, Georg Simmel and of course Karl Marx.

Of the three giants of classical sociology: the emotional Marx, the rational Durkheim and the sympathetic Weber, I rate Durkheim as first among equals. But it's a close call because, as I will argue later, in a crisis, irrational emotion must be able to brush aside objective rationality. So, it may be best to think of this 'greatest giant' competition as being triangular, or mutually trumping. Marx beats Durkheim, Durkheim beats Weber, Weber beats Marx. It doesn't seem to be a binary knockout competition: Marx > Durkheim > Marx > Durkheim . . .

Durkheim also put his finger on a key feature of group performance. I discuss his three types of 'anomie' in 'The Rule of Three'. (See PART 2 below).

Max Weber (1864–1920)

Weber was brought up in a prosperous Berlin family. He was a brilliant student who first studied law and then switched to economics. His health was never particularly good. He held posts at several major universities, and shortly before he died of pneumonia in 1920, he was made professor of sociology at Munich University.

Although they were the same age Weber and Durkheim seem to have had little to do with each other. As Calhoun puts it in *Classical Sociological Theory*:

> Weber and Durkheim were both part of a generation of turn-of-the-century academics who effectively founded sociology as a scientific endeavour. Weber was only a few years younger than his French counterpart, but he was a very different theorist in both style and substance. Although Weber most likely read Durkheim's work, he only made a few general remarks about the 'organic school' and in these he never mentioned Durkheim by name.

One ambition of Weber's sociology was to establish a value-free objective-scientific-sociology. 'Value free' was essential, but for him this sociology had to be able to deal with the unpleasant social consequences of its own objectivity. That is to say Weber strove to reconcile a strictly objective sociology in the scientific, *homo economicus* tradition of Adam Smith, with the humanist, *homo reciprocans* principles of J. J. Rousseau and Karl Marx.

J. H. Robb writing in *The Emergence of Social Theory* about the problem of establishing value-free sociology says:

> Because action has a subjective meaning to the actor (and perhaps to recipients or observers of the behaviour as well), it

cannot be simply observed and described in the way that is possible with data sources in the natural sciences; an attempt must be made to extract the meaning: it must be understood. This then gives the key to the question of how to make a scientific approach to data which differ from those of the natural sciences . . . in the case of the social sciences a causal explanation is incomplete and must be preceded by an interpretive explanation, an explanation based on *Verstehen* or the understanding of the meaning of the action to the actors involved.

Weber, in his book *Economy and Society*, published in 1922, explains what he means by *verstehen* (or meaningful understanding). The following comments were taken from Wikipedia in April 2018:

[*Verstehen* roughly means:] Interpretive or participatory examination of social phenomena – entering into the shoes of the other – to do research on actors without taking into account the meanings they attribute to their actions or environment is to treat them like objects.

Max Weber contributed several other ground-breaking concepts to sociology, these included that the Protestant Ethic in eighteenth-century Europe had created a fertile breeding ground for capitalism. Weber also praised bureaucracy as an efficient and rational way to organise human activity. But these contributions did not seek to reconcile *homo economicus* with his cousin *reciprocans*; they are outside the scope of what I am trying to say here about the proper unit of sociological study.

Of the three giants of modern sociology: Marx, Durkheim and Weber, Marx was emotional and highly political, Durkheim was analytically objective and deeply penetrating and Weber tried to reconcile these two different approaches with his concept of *verstehen*.

The Modern Schools after Marx, Durkheim and Weber

Between them Marx, Durkheim and Weber seemed to have said it all. And yet there was, and still is a lingering thought that there must be a 'science' in there somewhere, still waiting to be discovered. Or at least a definitive reconciliation between *homo economicus* and *homo reciprocans*, Seth Abrutyn's call in 2016 for a paradigm shift in sociology, (mentioned in my Introduction – page 24) says as much.

After this great trio, sociology fragmented into various schools based mainly in universities in North America and Europe. Intellectually the cutting edge became scattered all over the place. Here are some of the big names which crop up all the time: Sigmund Freud on sex and the unconscious, G. H. Mead a Chicago school empirical pragmatist, Antonio Gramsci an Italian anti-fascist, Emmeline Pankhurst on feminism, Herbert Marcuse a left-wing radical, Talcott Parsons a painstaking social theorist, Robert Merton on middle-range social theories, J. M. Keynes an economist, J. P. Sartre on existentialism, Simone de Beauvoir on feminism, Habermas on interpretation and communication and Bourdieu on structure and agency. The list goes on and on.

Talcott Parsons (1902–1979)

One of the most interesting sociologists is Talcott Parsons, an American who worked a lot in continental Europe. He developed an elaborate theory of social action in which he set his sights on the question of *how society works*. His target is almost the same as the one I aim at in this book. Guy Rocher on the very first page of his book *Talcott Parsons and American Sociology* (1972) says of Parsons: 'His entire work is directed towards a single objective: the development of a conceptual and theoretical framework intended to give sociology truly scientific status, and at the same time to relate it logically to the other social sciences.'

His stuff is famously hard to pin down but in a nutshell Talcott Parsons's general theory of social action may best be understood as coming in two parts: the structure of society and the processes of social behaviour; his structure underlying his processes.

In his *structural* part Parsons saw social theory, not quite the same thing as social reality, as coming in five layers of theory arranged in hierarchy. These were:

....

1. the top table, amenable to a general theory

2. theories on the motivations which drive *group* behaviours

3. theories about culture, public opinion, leadership etc., which make such groups tick

4. theories about particular *problem areas*

5. theories about these problem areas using statistical enquiries, surveys, etc.

....

In this cascade Parsons descends from theories about the top seat of society down to those about the individual person. He also used the notion that the top is mostly brain and the bottom is mostly brawn to establish a concept of society as a monolithic hierarchy amenable to statistics and mathematical modelling. This is essentially the raw material of *homo economicus*.

In his *processes*, the second part of Talcott Parsons's grand scheme, he describes how social units go about their work. For this he expounds his famous AGIL theory of social action, which is then superimposed on, or integrated across, these five layers of theory. This is like filling the squares on an imaginary chessboard.

And there we have it: this rather marvellous concept of theory laid crosswise upon theory constitutes Parsons's minutely analytical general theory of how society works. It's a complicated concept, and his tangled writing style doesn't help. It is a relief to find that I am not the only one who finds it all rather difficult.

Parsons's AGIL is clearly central to it all; it's about how labour-divided cooperating groups perform, explaining how they go about their work and the mechanisms of their behaviour.

A is adaptation. G is goals. I is integration. L is latency. On their own, these elements don't make much sense; they need considerable explanation. (In PART 2, I offer a translation that applies Assembly and Performance Thinking to these four functions. See *Translating Talcott Parsons's AGIL*.)

Guy Rocher describes the functions as follows:

A: adaptation. The biological organism corresponds to the function of adaptation.

G: goals. The personality corresponds to the function of goal attainment.

I: integration. The social system represents the function of integration.

L: latency: Culture represents the function of latency or pattern-maintenance.

Parsons used the metaphor, popular in rocket science, of 'cybernetic, negative feedback control loops.' These are integral in his structure of social action. They are the glue which amalgamates separate cooperating groups, each iterating their AGIL functions, into the monolith of society.

The word cybernetics makes these systems sound seriously scientific. But in fact, they occur all around us. Cybernetics is nothing more than a fancy name for simple control systems. A good example is the thermostat used in home central heating; it consists of a thermometer plus on/off switch. Dead simple; essentially the same as navigating a ship to harbour, controlling a guided missile to its target, or the herding of sheep by the farmer and his dog.

The reason why these feedback loops are called 'negative' is because they control down to zero – to a state of 'no difference' between their target and their actual position. They aim continually for stability or homeostasis. The all-important point here is that the target, the desired constant temperature for example, has to be set by somebody outside the loop. The 'plan, execute, review' control loop in assembly and performance thinking, referred to here as the rule of three, is quite different. It is self-motivated; its quasi-mind sets its own target. So, it is not a negative-feedback control loop. There is a big difference here which is further explained in PART 2 Performance.

Parsons's aim seems to have been that by rendering the individual, not the group, as the proper unit of analysis he would make sociology amenable to statistical economics and modelling. This classifies him as a homo economicus. His grand AGIL-plus-hierarchy system offers a theoretical structure to help us understand how society works. For a time during the 1940s and 1950s it was thought to be at the cutting edge of sociological theory, especially in the USA. But by 1970 it was no longer recognised to be the way forward. He was trapped by his own logic in a theoretical system, one which could not recognise the everyday social reality that labour-divided cooperating groups are self-motivating building blocks which rough-and-tumble about in the hierarchy of society like clothes in a washing machine.

From this argument Parsons's failure isn't because of his difficult writing style and his complex analysis. I think it is because his AGIL does not apply to self-motivated groups. Sadly, Parsons failed in his brave attempt 'to give sociology a truly scientific status and at the same time to relate it logically to the other social sciences'. To repeat this in different words: his cybernetic negative-feedback control loops must always have their targets set by external agents. This means that Parsons's model of society must always be a monolithic structure; it cannot be recognised as the real-life systems we all live in. The reality of human social life is that all over the world, from the Arctic Circle via South Africa to Malaysia and on through India to Patagonia, we live in self-motivated, selfishly ambitious, inter-connected amoral groups, each interacting interdependently in nested harmony – well it's usually harmonious. This is the subject of assembly and performance thinking examined in PART 2.

Talcott Parsons may not be one of the big names in sociology today, but as Stephen Mennell put it in his introduction to Guy Rocher's *Talcott Parsons and American Sociology*: 'Even if eventually one rejects Parsons's solutions, to study his ideas is an effective way to establish one's intellectual bearings – even though one may in the end side with his critics.'

Boredom

We all know the lifeless feeling of boredom. Also called listlessness or ennui, it gnaws away the daylight hours; eats them up. It can strike at the mother, worker and senior citizen, but the most vulnerable is the student. As I remember it boredom can tempt a capable youngster into alcohol, drugs, suicide, theft, and hooliganism. Its social aspect is alienation from the big wide world; not knowing where or how to fit in. To many students, boredom is one of the stark realities of social life. You're not much use on your own and finding a love-partner may help but it's certainly not the answer. You've somehow got to fit into the great hierarchy of life; the social rough and tumble going on right now, today, outside your door. And the good news is that you actually are wanted.

Here for the student is the answer from assembly and performance thinking:

Ignoring everybody around – parents, friends, everybody – identify the activities which excite you most.

Which of them are you best at?

Sort these according to most needed in society.

Pursue the one that tops your list. It should be your main career.

Then the rest can be your life-long hobbies. They can be your answers to boredom so enjoy them with vigour. They can even get you out of unemployment.

The Building Block Question: *homo economicus* or *homo reciprocans*?

OK, so which is the better unit to use as your building block when constructing your idea of society: what is it really and how does it work? Should you use the individual, the raw material of statistics, or the working group as your unit? Or should it be mixtures of both? There is still no consensus on this. Economic theory almost bridges the gap, but it can't, because economic man isn't altruistic. He – it is always he, never she – is endowed with a standard set of wants and needs and these don't include altruism, emotion or discretion. And *homo reciprocans* isn't amenable to statistics; we can't yet measure altruism, emotion or discretion. Despite centuries of trying we still cannot measure happiness.

Maybe one day this *economicus* v. *reciprocans* riddle will be solved but right now the thoughtful student puts it all away in the 'too difficult' box. She has been sitting exams on the great men like Confucius, Jesus, Socrates, Epicurus, Mohammed, Rousseau, Smith, Comte, Durkheim, Marx, Lenin, Hegel, Webber, Spencer, Parsons, and many more, But she does notice that sociologists seldom if ever agree among themselves, and that few have been able to stitch Darwin's natural selection into their theories. She realises that if only these great men could have built on each other's work like scientists have always done, sociology would be much easier to master.

Here ends The Student's Tale.

Emily the fair
Joyfully washed her body in a well
But how she did her rite I dare not tell
Save in a general way, though I for one
Think that the detail would be fun.
If one means well why bother to be queasy?
It's good for people to be free and easy.
Her shining hair untressed her cloak
They combed and set a crown of cerrial oak
Green on her head with fitting grace

From *The Knight's Tale*, Geoffrey Chaucer

THE APPRENTICE'S TALE

The Audit Clerk

The carefree days of the student are over. The apprentice, unsure what social life is about, finds that his or her horizons have been reduced. Whatever the world may be, it is no longer her oyster. Ambitions are restricted by the shock of long hours at work in law offices, on building sites, in hospitals, factory floors, firms of accountants or school classrooms, or in the apprenticeship of motherhood. This at last is the real world and for some it is beset with tough exams.

I passed out of TCD in 1953, a pimply youth with second-class honours. I soon stopped wondering who I was supposed to be because in January 1954 I was apprenticed to Stokes Brothers and Pim, a Dublin firm of chartered accountants. They were Protestants with strong Quaker connections. But the apprentice is young and strong, and if he gets out of bed early enough there's still time for fun. In my case that meant painting, sailing, rowing and going to parties.

In my four long years as a junior – you didn't become a senior till you passed the final exams – I went out on audits all over the place: Findlater's, the family grocers, Bewley's Oriental Cafés, Player's Cigarettes and Dunlop Tyres. Typically, an audit lasted about a month.

On arrival at the client's office we were ushered, with ceremony, into a dauntingly important private room. Accounting records would be brought in for us on request and the audit would begin. We set to work checking and ticking off numbered sheaves of sales dockets, carefully ordered receipt books and petty-cash vouchers, purchases and sales ledgers and bank statements. We traced these figures carefully into ledgers. Also called daybooks, these were beautifully bound with proper stitch-binding; loose-leaf ledgers had not yet been invented. We totted up columns of figures and cross-checked totals to control-accounts and thence to the great 'journal of prime entry'. We used an assortment of different ticks. These were somewhat like naval signals used at sea. One said you had checked the origin of a figure, another that you had checked its destination, one that you had totted up a column of figures or a cross-tot, which was not the same as a cross-check, and a mark to show you had double-checked these. On and on we went: from there to the trial balance, and finally, in great secrecy, to the profit and loss account and balance sheet, at which point the audit was finished and our working papers were ready for examination by the audit partner. This was always a daunting experience; you wore your best suit when the audit partner reviewed your working papers.

The client's accounting staff had usually been articled clerks in their day, and it was customary to be given a present at the end of an audit: a big box of cigarettes from John Player's, which my mother appreciated, and assorted goodies from Jacob's Biscuits. Every week on the Jameson's Whiskey audit I gave my mother advance warning that I might come home slightly tiddly after the regular Friday session we were expected to attend in the tasting room.

During the audit of Newsoms – 'The Gentlemen's Outfitters' – in Mullingar, Protestants of course, I was booked in at the Catholic hotel, not the Protestant one. It was explained to me later that this was because if one did happen to gossip in the Catholic hotel about Newsoms' affairs it was unlikely to spread into the Protestant community. I bought a very nice pair of leather boots at a knock-down price at the end of the audit. The hotel, which was attached to the town abattoir, served the most delicious lamb chops I have ever tasted anywhere, before or since. The waitress said, 'Ah yea, dat'll be da ryga martice.' She explained that the trick is to get the chop into the frying-pan before it's had time to go stiff. 'Der's not many as knows dat,' she said.

On the audit of Barry's – 'Tea Merchants since 1901' – in Cork, we would be ceremoniously installed under a portrait of the founder. The company books would be brought in and the fire would be lit with quiet precision. That was in 1955 and it was proudly explained to us that the coal was from a still remaining consignment of Chinese coal the company had imported before the First World War. The board room and the coal were only used for the Annual General Meeting and the auditors' visit.

I was painfully innocent; it took me half an hour reading the thick accountancy textbook by Pickles and Dunkerley before I could understand what an invoice was, and another half hour mastering its legal significance as a 'voucher'. 'A contract is a legally binding agreement between two parties', and all that. It was hard to believe that something so ridiculously simple could be so important in the great commercial world I had just entered.

My very first outing was on what was called a 'surprise cash-count' at a big hotel in Bray, eighteen miles south of Dublin. I was told to check the petty cash. Several cashboxes were in use, and the idea was that between them there had, at any time, to be either cash or vouchers amounting to a round sum, say £50. It was called the 'imprest system' and I couldn't work it out at all. Reggie Crampton, the senior on the job said, 'Oh for goodness! sake Wilson! Here, give it to me.' But he couldn't work it out either. Later that week there was some private talking and I learnt that the cashier, a nice elderly lady, was to be sacked. She'd been fiddling the petty cash. Bit of a shock. Reggie told us later that when he asked her to explain the deficit she'd simply said, 'Ah sit down and have a cup of tea.' Of course, we keen young apprentices were eager to make our name by uncovering a fraud, but that was my only one, and on my very first audit. The reality of it was not very nice at all and, looking back I'm glad I never uncovered another. There were better ways to make your reputation.

After I qualified as a proud member of the Institute of Chartered Accountants in Ireland, which, by the way covered both North and South, I went to work for the European branch of Price Waterhouse, headquartered in Paris. It was a big international firm of Chartered Accountants. This was not long after the war, and reconstruction money was pouring into Western Europe. The Americans were buying up businesses in France, Germany, Italy and Spain. The various European languages and accounting methods were alien to Americans, and they wanted to know what they were investing in; they needed to investigate and then to audit the books of target businesses. So, the big English audit firms were crying out for newly qualified young chartered accountants who could stumble through one or two foreign languages. Like me from Dublin. Others came from Cardiff, Glasgow, Manchester, Leeds and Belfast. We quickly became friends, found that we were surprisingly well paid, and had a high old time.

Our Apprenticeship Was Unique

The overall pattern of each audit was always the same. Looking back now I can see that it was invariably a review of the *performance* of a social unit: a mini society, sometimes a very big one, in which individuals *assembled* and shared their skills altruistically to produce goods or services. It is clear that these goods or services always contributed in one way or another to satisfy the nationwide will to survive and prosper; the will which motivates us to Metabolise (take on energy and eliminate waste), Self-protect and Reproduce.

It is true of course that apprentice doctors, lawyers, geologists and engineers had to take a similar plunge into the deep end of life, but there were two unique things about being an articled clerk in a firm of chartered accountants. One was that we had to master the logic of double-entry bookkeeping. That was not too difficult, after all medical students had to master the workings of the human body, but the other was that we innocent youths were sent out to verify the commercial secrets of the biggest employers in the country. Typically, one went out on about ten audits per year.

Sadly, the wider social significance of all this passed me by. The only unique thing about bookkeeping I noticed at the time was that it has three double letters in a row, but that just got me suspicious looks.

The key to double-entry bookkeeping is its rather amazing logic. The books always had to balance after every entry and if they didn't, we had to chase figures through the books, checking columns of figures and carry-overs between books to find out why. This could be a headache, but we got good at it, learning tricks like seeing did the difference come to 9 or a multiple of 9. Because, if so, the mistake was almost certain to be a transposed carry-over, where, for example, someone had put 32 instead of 23. The worst ones were where the difference was made up of two or more errors. There were no computers in those days; it was all pencil and rubber, ruler and paperclip. English speakers might like to know that the French for paperclip is 'trombone' – because of its resemblance to that lovely musical instrument.

We had to get it into our young heads that this terrifying logic was invariably the same in each and every audit. No matter how different the industry, be it transport, steel-working, publishing, advertising or hotels, the logic was always the same. And not only that, but this logic always amounted to a working model. That's to say it could be used in much the same way as admiralty charts and road maps are used to simulate the outcomes of alternative decisions without actually making the journey or learning how others have already done it.

Budgetary control, promoted since the 1920s by J. O. McKinsey in his classic textbook with the same name, compares trends in actual performance with ambition. It enables the business manager to do 'what-ifs' about future outcomes of different decisions about pricing, product development, remuneration policies, capital investment and so on. These simulations are in effect trial-and-error feedback-control loops not unlike the cybernetic systems used in rocket science. I have already referred to them under Talcott Parsons above. You select your target, set your course, go, record progress against target, and adjust your course, as necessary. Budgetary control relies on cleanly disciplined double-entry bookkeeping, and double-entry bookkeeping is what we youngsters were sent out to audit.

It is only recently that I have come to realise what a very special apprenticeship we articled clerks in firms of chartered accountants actually received. Buddha, Socrates, Aristotle, Christ, Averroes, Descartes, Bacon, Hume, Kant, Wittgenstein – they had all been brilliant youngsters who effortlessly stored away and pondered the rich experiences of social life, but none of them spent seven years as privileged pimply youths prying into the workings of the most successful businesses of their day. And more than that; none of them were trained to apply a universal working model which through the medium of money fitted every one of their business corporations. The leading philosophers and sociologists of today still do not seem to have recognised the wider implication of all this.

But there it is: through the use of money to facilitate trade, medieval merchants invented double-entry bookkeeping. This is a universal model which fits one of the most common species of human groups, the monetarised business. I don't know what percentage of the world's population can be counted as working in these units, from little rowing clubs via criminal gangs and government departments to giant multi-nationals, but it must be close to eighty per cent because most of us work in more than one.

Monetisation

Karl Marx did not invent the word 'capitalism', but he gave it a good boost. He emphasised both its historical inevitability and its potential nastiness. Like it or not, many of the things Marx said have come to pass. Thanks to Marx a shrill debate between socialism and capitalism still assails the ears of the twenty-first-century apprentice.

It may be useful to remember that money is the engine-oil of capitalism. Being social animals, we are bartering with each other all day long, making deals. So too are honeybees, ants, killer whales and naked mole-rats. When quid-pro-quo deals are made between killer whales, memory greatly enhances their cooperation. The social insects have more primitive but similarly functioning systems. We humans have developed the use of money, or tokens, to extend this transactional memory in regularly recurring deals. Money even enables us to by-pass these memories. We use money to facilitate most of the three main functions of life, metabolization, self-protection and breeding. The dowry tradition is one of the oldest ways in which human breeding deals have been monetised. Substantial tokens have always been traded during betrothals and always will be. We have even been able to monetise many aspects of warfare.

In the 1960s and 1970s my wife and I regularly took our three little children on holiday to Leenane. It was a little village of about fifteen houses on the west coast of Ireland. The extended population, when it gathered for weddings, funerals and fairs, numbered about 500 and was made up of farmers, fishing folk and holidaymakers like us.

There were two general stores side by side, Hamiltons and Gaynors, each with a crowded pub in the back smelling of turf-smoke and stale Guinness. There were two churches: one Catholic and one Protestant, a tiny harbour and a petrol pump. There was one TV set, owned by a farmer up on the Leenane mountain; it was used for watching the Galway races and for Gaelic football. We watched the first moon landing on it. The weather was wild, the sea was tremendous and rich with Atlantic sea-life. It rained a lot.

Everybody knew everybody else and memories were long. Favours were given, remembered, and returned over intervals measured by harvests, salmon-runs and sheep-shearing. There were a few tractors and trucks around, but Eddie Hamilton, the village entrepreneur, was about the only one who had a saloon car. He knew when anyone needed a lift, to the doctor in Westport, the dentist in Clifden or to mass on Sunday. He was very generous about it, seldom accepting money.

In fact, money was not used very much at all. Pints of Guinness were often traded by memory or favour-exchange, or they were added on to the 'page' system which was used extensively for groceries. When the time came to pay for anything a pen had to be found, items remembered, listed and totted up. The till had to be opened. It made a loud 'ting!' Everything else had to stop, but it was a nice moment for repartee, thanks and 'Mind how you go now.'

Of course, since those days Leenane has gradually been monetised; the automatic till and the credit card now rule OK. We all shudder at the stunningly sterilising, ever-creeping, apparently unstoppable process of monetisation. It's a process which takes over, sanitises, brands and homogenises our best little enterprises; I'm referring to the vibrant activities we used to perform in small assembled groups, and whose human warmth we regularly kill with the dead hand of creeping monetisation and its smiling henchman, marketing. This is the apparently unstoppable march of the corporates. Examples include local fisheries, family restaurants, pop groups, local veterinary practices and sports events. Few people have ever put this better than Joni Mitchell in her haunting 1970 song, *Big Yellow Taxi*: 'Don't it always seem to go / That you don't know what you've got till it's gone / They paved paradise / And put up a parking lot.'

It seems possible that the most inhuman consequences of monetisation might have been avoided if social theorists like Karl Marx, *homo reciprocans* though he was, had been quicker to notice that the group, not the individual, is the proper unit for the study of society and that the profit-and-loss account and balance sheet is a ready-made simulation-model of every single one of these monetised groups. They just need the same rules for all, a level playing-field, and legal control. All three of which they readily accept. All this has been under our very noses ever since double-entry bookkeeping, with its two o's, two k's and two e's, was first invented around a thousand years ago independently in Korea and Genoa.

Have We Missed a Trick?

Could it be that ever since the world's first monasteries and universities we have always seduced our brightest young brains, our Aristotles and Durkheims, into the prestigious halls of academia before they have lived enough of the rough and tumble of life out in the real world? This may be the best way to explain why the privileged social experiences gained by the young articled clerk in a firm of Chartered Accountants do not seem to have transferred across to the doctrines of social theory. And yet here we have a remarkably powerful social simulation tool: a one hundred and fifty-year-old body of expertise which models the feedback mechanisms at work in the most important type of building block making up the hierarchy of modern society. Financial models are powerful navigational tools for recording past performance and plotting the best course to steer on. They show how each one of these mini societies works.

But there is a trap here. Money, chased for its own sake, sings a siren song which usually ends in misery. Heaven forbid that we should ever try to monetise society. Ferdinand Tonnies put his finger on the answer to all this; he gave us the nod that though it may be wise to monetise the business-type *Gesellschafts* of society, we should never do it to our family-type *Gemeinschafts*; and that we need to recognise the difference between the two.

None of us saw it that way at the time, but in retrospect it becomes obvious that we fresh-faced apprentice Chartered Accountants, boys and girls, were dealing all along with mini societies, some quite small, others big. And in doing so we were using a universally applicable working model of the labour-divided, monetised working group: the commonest species in the whole social jungle. With this in mind it may be possible to improve our understanding of society simply by recognising that cooperating groups, rather than individuals, are its proper building blocks. In other words, by recognising that these blocks are the only units of which our raucous society is constructed. These ideas are further developed in PART 2 below.

Here endeth The Apprentice's Tale.

> Many a ledger and money bag he got
> And laid them out upon his counting board
> He had a deal of treasure in his hoard
> And so he locked the door with an abrupt
> Command that no one was to interrupt
> His casting of accounts; he worked away
> Sitting up there till past the prime of day.

From *The Shipman's Tale*, Geoffrey Chaucer

THE MOTHER'S TALE

Having considered social reality as it appears to the child, the student and then to the apprentice, let's now look at it from the mother's angle. She doesn't have much time for philosophy; her angle on reality is that if it looks like a duck, walks like a duck and quacks like a duck then it is a duck.

The mother is practical; she doubts both the idealistic student and the male-dominated tough-guy world of the apprentice. She brings a touch of humanism. Having babies does that to us all. It is at the very heart of society.

She is now in her mid thirties, embodies common sense and enjoys a good gossip. Though men can be a bit of a joke she is not exactly cynical, motherhood has made her too well balanced for that. She is realistic and down-to-earth, she punctures male fantasy, but she does it with a feather not with a pin. As well as loving a good party the mother is sometimes awake at 3 a.m. feeding her baby; she does the shopping and the cooking. She cleans the house and she gets the children dressed and ready for school. In fact, this slim young person floating about, effortlessly carrying a toddler on her hip, is a good deal more resilient than she ever thought she was. This all-round toughness is seldom recognised in the public imagination, which prefers to admire the testosterone-fuelled ruggedness of young men, outdoors or behind the steering-wheel.

The tales of the child, student, apprentice, worker and senior citizen are gender-neutral, everybody is included: heterosexual men and women and the LGBTQs. The Mother's Tale is unavoidably gender-specific and, being a man, I am a bit out of my depth here, but I will try to describe the mother's angle on how society really works.

The History of Hubris

The mother looks on the doings of men with an indulgent smile; left on their own they can make a hopeless mess of things. Masculine self-importance or hubris, instilled from birth, is usually the reason. This is the belief that, through God, the human is the centre of the universe. Or, as the ancient Greek philosopher Protagoras famously put it, 'Man is the measure of all things.' But where did this daft idea come from?

Hubris is the Ancient Greek word for impertinence towards the gods. It was one of the themes in Homer's epic stories the *Iliad* and the *Odyssey*. Plato's cosmology, written down four hundred years after Homer, was classic hubris and it still lies deep in our folklore. Some of the wilder proposals in today's religions can be traced back to Plato's famous metaphor of the cave, which said that reality exists in an ethereal 'other' place.

Two thousand years after Plato along came Darwin, who banged our heads together, pointing out that we are descended from monkeys. It gradually became obvious from what Darwin had said, that the assembly of individual creatures into altruistic members of working teams is a major achievement in evolutionary terms; one which is not unique to humans. But we are the dominant creature on our planet, and we are, even today, still dazzled by the brilliance of our own reflection. I blame Plato, but it had started long before him. Plato built his glorious cosmology on Pythagoras and Parmenides, among others. It's a pity he ignored Homer because Plato's cosmology, clearly, is simple, pure hubris. Here, taken from F. M. Cornford's translation, is a summary of what Plato said in the *Timaeus* about reality:

The real world we experience through our senses is so messy, changeable and random that the truth cannot be found there; it is the inferior world of 'sensible' things.

There is a superior world of ideas apparent in mathematics and geometry, which is eternal; it is timeless. It pre-exists life. To create an image of the eternal world, one where humans could live, God had to invent time, and time then gave rise to number.

This enabled God to copy everything down into the inferior world. He copied the ideal forms existing in the superior world. He added that in copying, mistakes can sometimes get made. This was his brilliant get-out clause.

So here we have Plato, an intelligent animal, trying to make sense of things that are beyond its intellectual capacity. The inevitable result is that it ends up inventing an all-powerful God in its own image.

Thus, Plato's gloriously homocentric and all-explaining rationalisation assumed the existence of a higher realm of eternal mathematical principles and ideal forms. This then became the basis for Judaism, Christianity and Islam: the city-based religions of the Western World. And although much altered and frequently split by schisms, it still underlies Western culture today. God still lives up there in the sky.

Plato's internally consistent reality-consolidation of contemporary mathematics, theology and folklore is absolutely brilliant. But there's not a single shred of empirical evidence for it; it is quite obviously total nonsense.

But then Georg Hegel went even further, writing: 'Man is not sharply distinct from God but rises to God over the course of history'; there's hubris for you, in the raw.

Hubris is essentially a disease of the tribe not the individual. Personally, I'm proud to be a member of the group, but it is 'we' who are the greatest, not I on my own, and as the mother points out, this belief has a masculine, chest-beating voice.

The astonishing advances in modern science and technology – in space exploration, genetics, medicine and quantum mechanics – when coupled with our inherent religiosity, make it difficult not to believe in the Godlike superiority of *Homo sapiens*. There it stands, like the Tower of Babel built on centuries of the accumulated detritus of human habitation, there is the holy shrine of our self-importance.

Things/Non-Things and Humility: a re-setting to remove hubris

Since Darwin's day and the publication of *On the Origin of Species* in 1859, it has been understood that the human is an animal 'descended from monkeys.' In comparison with the simplest worm, we may indeed be supremely evolved but so is the leaf-cutter ant: it too has invented agriculture. Other spectacular life forms which may help to put us in our place include the cunning octopus, which being a mollusc is closely related to slugs. There's the naked mole-rat, a mammal which has developed an elaborate underground social life involving, rather amazingly, a breeding queen. And then there's the slime-mould: an individual single-celled amoeba which cooperates with other individuals to travel and to breed. As in ants this creature's cooperativeness includes a readiness for self-sacrifice for the good of the group. The human is merely another cooperating animal.

If we were able with due humility to abandon our deep-seated belief in the unique supremacy of mankind, we might get a clearer understanding of our animal nature and therefore of how society works, but the problem here is that the obstacle of hubris is massive, and like Nietzsche it despises humility. Maybe we should go right back to basics and start all over again.

In The Child's Tale the cognitive primacy of things over non-things seemed clear. Those *things* ranging from worms to stars which we perceive by seeing, hearing, feeling, tasting and smelling are more primitive and compelling, more *real*, than the secondary impressions, the opinions and explanations, which are processed and interpreted by our intellect. I refer to the latter here as *non-things*. Emile Durkheim, writing in 1895, (*The Rules of Sociological Method*) said: 'A thing is any object of knowledge which is not normally penetrable by the under-standing.' In other words, Durkheim wanted to deal in measurable, primary, social realities; he didn't want to be messed about by the secondary products of the intellect. He wanted to avoid the introspective turbulence of philosophy in the intellectual stratosphere where the Oozlum bird plays.

Differentiating Things from Non-Things

But non-things can be surprising. If we define them as objects of enquiry which vanish when the human interpreting intellect is absent, then numbers and mathematics must be non-things. Maybe we need more thought here. For example, even if our brains deceive us by wrongly interpreting a thing perceived by our senses that thing is still a thing, and the interpretation we give it is still a non-thing. The distinction between things and non-things is not altered by mistaken identity.

A non-thing is not a thing at all; it's a negative. Michelangelo's *Pietà*, the Virgin Mary cradling the dead body of Christ, is a non-thing; only the marble it is made of is a thing. This re-setting falsifies Plato's widely accepted notion that truth or reality can only be found in the unchanging world of ideal forms, and that even then it is discernible only by the human intellect. It falsifies Plato's confirmation that 'humans are special'.

This re-setting is intellectually crude; its purpose is just to side-step theology and philosophy; to set them aside as hindrances to straight thinking about human society. It's not to say that they are wrong, just that they get in the way.

Religion and God are natural human social constructs and, as will be explained below, they retain a proud place in this 'things/non-things re-setting; though God vanishes when the human intellect is absent and is therefore a 'non-thing', religion in its temples, cathedrals, priests, rituals and congregations do not; these religious manifestations are 'things'.

It now gets complicated because the rejection of Plato's 'higher-lower realms of reality' idea and the putting in its place of the 'things /

non-things distinction' still remains valid when there is nobody around to notice. Thus, anybody wanting to argue that this re-setting is false or trivial must be able to show that their alternative reality is equally valid when there is nobody around to notice. Alternatively, they must accept that their 'higher-lower' idea fails this test because it is a product of the human intellect. They must recognise that the 'things/ non-things argument bypasses, is not subject to, does not require, human interpretation. A biologist studying chimpanzees can only work with the objectively observable 'things' of the case; if chimpanzees have philosophy it would not be relevant; observable 'things' are all there is to go on. It's the same with humans; human reasoning is irrelevant here because the viewpoint is strictly objective. As Ronald Knox impiously wrote:

> There once was a man who said, 'God
> Must think it exceedingly odd
> If he finds that this tree
> Continues to be
> When there's no one about in the Quad.'
> This was God's reply:
> 'Dear Sir, Your astonishment's odd;
> I am always about in the Quad
> And that's why the tree
> Will continue to be
> Since observed by
> Yours faithfully, God.'

This things, non-things distinction is not difficult, but one must first abandon the thought that eternal or *a priori* principles are the ultimate reality underlying social life. It is only Plato's cosmology which complicates. A one-year-old child has a good grasp of the reality of the senses, it is not until it is about three that the questions about life begin. At this point it is given answers which date back to well before Plato. In the fourteenth century, William of Ockham expounded the principle now known as Ockham's razor, that if you wish to choose between two competing explanations it is best to choose the simpler one. By this test it seems better to base your thinking on what we can all actually see, hear and touch than on human interpretations thereof.

Things/Non-Things: more examples

Things are those objects of enquiry which 'continue to be when there's no one about in the quad'. But cultural conventions are essential for the smooth functioning of society, and they are so powerful that they can often blur the edges. They are so powerful that we occasionally fool ourselves into thinking that the products of the intellect are real things. There are lots of border-line cases. I was overcome by emotion when I first saw Michelangelo's *Pietà* in St Peter's Basilica in Rome; did a human actually carve that out of one block of marble? I wanted to touch it. It was one of the most electric experiences of my life. I had to go back again the following day. But to a wild horse it would just be a lump of white stone in a sheltered place. This view ridicules questions like: Is it real or in my head? and: Is it still there at night when nobody's looking? But an art historian might need the promptings of child-like innocence to get it from the horse's view. The statue is a non-thing whereas the stone is a thing. Morality is another example. We can watch selective self-restraint happening among wolves and chimpanzees as well as humans. It looks like a real thing, but morality is just our way of explaining the counter-intuitive compulsion to self-restraint in humans; the behaviour is a thing but the morality of it is a non-thing.

Here are some more examples which may help to illustrate the distinction. A thing does not need to have a non-thing counterpart; we only cook these up when we feel the need for explanations, for example think of a stone. A small stone on the ground requiring no explanation normally has no non-thing counterpart, unless of course we start wondering about it, where did it come from? Why is it there? What's it made of? Historians, geologists and geographers may then populate the realm of non-things with their explanations. It is a question of how important, useful or exciting we consider the item to be in everyday life.

Manchester United is a non-thing. Its players, supporters, stadium and T-shirts are things, but the club is a non-thing.

Natural selection is a non-thing; it may work but it is an explanation made by humans.

A business corporation is a non-thing; its products and facilities are things and so are its members.

Consciousness is a non-thing; being aware that you are aware is also a non-thing.

Cohesive behaviour and the group quasi-mind only exist as concepts in the mind of the human observer; they are non-things and have no thing-counterparts.

With apologies to Plato, straight lines, numbers, geometry, mathematics and 2 + 2 = 4 are non-things.

God is a non-thing; she or he vanishes in the absence of the human interpreting intellect.

What about time? It seems difficult to understand what time actually is, when did it start, or did it ever start? Is the 'space-time continuum' a thing? What was there before time began? For the limited purpose of this essay, which is to elucidate the mechanisms of human society, I hope it's enough to file time in the drawer marked 'philosophy', with a note attached saying 'probably a non-thing'.

Models and maps are difficult; are they things or non-things? The Mediterranean Sea is still there when there is nobody to look at it, it is clearly a thing. A map of the Mediterranean, consisting of paper and ink is also a thing. But its use as a model to simulate sea voyages is a non-thing.

The Mother Sidesteps Philosophy

This distinction between 'things' and 'non-things' is sharply different from the philosophers' distinction between physics and metaphysics. Kant called them phenomena and noumena. Rodin's statue *The Thinker*, a heroic man, not a woman of course, comes to mind here. Philosophers seek to establish the elusive fundamental truths about the world, they ask what reality *is*, what to be *means*, what *are* time and infinity, what life *is*, and so on.

The following definitions are taken from the *Penguin Dictionary of Philosophy* (2000 edition), edited by Thomas Maunter:

> Epistemology: Theory of knowledge; the branch of philosophy that enquires into the nature and possibility of knowledge.

Ontology: Inquiry into, or theory of, being *qua* being.

Hermeneutics: Inquiry into, or theory of, the nature of methods of interpretation.

It is only when thinking about one's own self that these questions become interesting. Each of these great fields of philosophical enquiry delves into the mind of the individual thinker; not, as I do here, into the very much more primitive mind of the group. After all, groups only have quasi-minds. When thinking about the reality of social life these questions don't seem relevant.

The things / non-things distinction promoted here has a more mundane and restrictive purpose, which is to understand the mechanisms of society, not of the cosmos. This distinction merely defends the treatment of humans as animals against any objections coming from philosophy or religion. Groups don't introspect, and I must repeat that when examining the Rule of Three I'm talking about the workings of the group mind, not the mind of an individual. Taking the down-to-earth mother's view of society: philosophy no longer holds the intellectual high-ground, *Homo sapiens* no longer occupy the centre of the universe, primary reality side-steps Plato's cosmology, and it becomes easier to disregard the ontological, hermeneutical, epistemological introspections of philosophy.

The mother's distinction between things and non-things is played out down here on earth, not somewhere up in heaven. This little verse says it nicely:

Inside our Dreams
Where do people go to when they die?
Somewhere down below or in the sky?
'I can't be sure,' said granddad, 'but it seems
They simply set up home inside our dreams.'

From *Toffee Pockets* (1992) by Jeanne Willis

Some More Mothers' Tales: law-making, leadership and emotion

The mother's main message is about hubris. But women have been subservient to men for centuries, so it's not surprising they have a few more things to say. For example, about law-making, leadership and emotion.

Law-making

Why does the law have to be such a dreadful muddle? It's different in every country you visit. In the British Isles the institutions, interpretation and execution of law are so hopelessly intertwined that nobody other than lawyers understands how it works. The rest of us don't know the differences between criminal and civil offences, between solicitors and barristers, between statute law and case law, between property law and divorce law, and that's just scratching the surface. The result is that we need highly qualified and expensive professionals to explain to us how it works before we can even begin. An enormous amount of the nation's brainpower is diverted into this unproductive process.

The English legal system has grown organically out of ancient Roman law, and it is now in such a colossal muddle that we all sense that since it seems to work OK it's probably best not to tinker with it.

But, the mother wonders, does it really have to be like that? Until the twentieth century law-making in the West was essentially a man-thing. The mother's angle was to let them get on with it, but if the woman-in-the-street ever gets worked up about it as she did in the French Revolution, the law could well be given a thorough spring clean. Some basic ideas about where to start are lightly outlined in 'The law: separating individual from group law' in PART 3 below.

Leadership and Emotion; who runs the show?

Men are quick to claim the social high ground where they can strut and show off like Colonel Hathi, the loveable patriarch in charge of the Pachyderm Parade in the Walt Disney classic, *The Jungle Book* (1967). He leaves questions of emotion, morale and family harmony to his wife Winifred, but the question of social power can become an issue when there is a serious threat to the group's food supply, its self-protection or breeding arrangements. At that point, the group's existing constitution gets tested. That is when, triggered by fear, anger or disgust, the potential force of emotion can kick its way in.

Emotion can easily override rationality. It is dangerous; it can upset the status quo. Emotion can trigger rebellion and destroy a group, and as the mother knows very well, women are better at it than men. There is a tendency, one could call it the Nietzsche effect, to dislike emotion; to ignore it as cissy, undignified, ignoble, an embarrassing personal character flaw; above all to recognise emotion as a threat to teamwork.

That may well be so, but in a conflict, the group which is alerted more quickly by the electrifying power of emotion will have a distinct advantage over its competitor. Emotion is thus recognised as a vitally essential social function. Nietzsche's will to power, which despises emotion as feminine, is thus seen to be naively unbalanced, narrowly masculine and hubristic.

In human affairs it's a good thing that the emotional response is more often used as an alert signal than it is used as a banner for action. The mother recognises that it is the men not the women who get killed in war. She has a generous and loving nature and is normally content with the idea that men like Colonel Hathi should run the show, but only because she knows that when it matters it is the women who pull the strings. And the men who get killed.

The mother is most certainly not a feminist, but the warning is clear; societies which listen properly to their women have a long-term advantage over those that do it less well.

> In company she loved to laugh and chat
> And knew the remedies for life's mischances,
> An art in which she knew the oldest dances.

From *The Prologue*, Geoffrey Chaucer

THE EMPLOYEE'S TALE

Let's see what social reality looks like from the employee's point of view.

I became an employee, an industrial accountant, immediately after the Second World War. We found ourselves in companies which were run on military lines. We were recruited by retired colonels and admirals and it took us some years respectfully to push these splendid men into accepting less paternalistic, more democratic management methods. In financial departments all over the Western world this meant altering the primary purpose of accounting which up till then had consisted of reporting to the shareholders and preparing tax returns. Battles took place between shareholder reporting and budgetary control.

I was in the thick of all this. After six years working for Price Waterhouse in Europe I had come over to England and, from 1965 to 1987, worked as financial controller, a new job title in those days, in big British-owned multi-national corporations. One after the other I worked for the Avon Rubber Company, Guest Keen & Nettlefolds (GKN), and British Oxygen (BOC). In each of these I had to strive for authority over the traditional accounting department before I could bring about the necessary changes.

The shareholder and the taxman would always be important, not to mention the banker and lawyer, but as we tried to point out, these must always take second place to the vital, forward-looking task of navigation in the face of tough competition, often from abroad. Go too fast and the business could go bust; too slow and you could be swallowed up by a competitor.

I was supported by like-minded bosses: managing directors whose job titles gradually changed to 'chief executive'. Business-management theory was developing fast, and British industry was in decline. I was sacked twice in management upheavals. It was an exciting ride.

We're All Employees

Employees include farm-lads, seamstresses, waitresses, sailors, prime ministers, field marshals, judges and doctors. But children, students, mothers and senior citizens are not employees, nor are poets, saints, rebels, criminals or vagabonds, and neither are slaves.

Employees are monetised. They can even be bought and sold. They can be thought of as hoards or millions of people. From this angle employees are expendable. In a war they become the cannon-fodder, millions of faceless people. You see them at railway stations and airports moving like ants. Employees service the social nest. That is their purpose.

The other way of seeing employees, the view taken in this tale, is as team players. They get their identity from the team, corporation, nation and race they belong to. They are individuals who have become cogs in working units, in teams or nations.

These units then rough-and-tumble about, as units; they are amalgamations not individuals. They produce the goods and services needed by the social nest to metabolise, self-protect and breed. This rough-and-tumble settles itself naturally into the hierarchy we think of as society.

An individual employee plays a specific part in its team, a role. This applies to wolves and dolphins as well as to humans. And though each human team is a separate unit with recognisable boundaries and members, individuals usually have roles in more than one team. This adds a wonderful complexity to our social life; it is elegantly displayed by Social Network Analysis (SNA). How it all works is the subject of PART 2 below.

Role play has been extensively analysed in sociology. For example, by Florian Znaniecki (1882–1958), a Polish sociologist active after the First World War in Poland and in America where he worked with W. I. Thomas and the Chicago School. In his *The Method of Sociology* (1934), Znaniecki said:

> The sociologist must take the human individual not as he 'really is' organically and psychologically, but as he is made by others and himself to appear in their experience and his own in the case of his social relationships.

As well as working, the employee always has time for play and for thinking. The inevitability of death comes quietly into the frame for the first time, not in a morbid sense, simply as being inevitable; it's just a background reality to The Employee's Tale. Up to now, mortality hasn't really been given too much thought by the child, student, apprentice or mother.

The Nature of Groups

Groups have ambition and purpose. Like the swirling flocks of starlings, you sometimes see, or the shoals of little fish all pointing one way under piers, or herds of migrating wildebeest, groups have body. They have a body which is more unified and purposeful than clouds, or smoke, or even river currents. Groups are animated by a common purpose, ambition or will. They look mindless but they're not. Human groups can and often do set out with purpose to kill or to destroy, and there's the difference: crowds at busy railway stations don't do that.

Wilfred Bion (1897–1979)

Wilfred Bion was an Englishman born in India. He had a brave and distinguished military career, earning both the British DSO and the French Croix d'Honneur in the First World War. At the end of the Second World War in which Bion had served in the Royal Army Medical Corps, he got together with several others who were interested in psychiatry to pool their experiences in the British Army. They founded the Tavistock Institute of Human Relations which is still going strong today. Their aim was to develop for civilians the knowledge of mental disorders they had gained in warfare.

Bion pioneered the technique known as group therapy in which it is the group not the individual which comes under the spotlight. The idea is that in this way the individual member learns from intensive interaction with, and criticism from, his or her peers. Thus, each person learns how others see them, where their personality is socially awkward, and receives advice on how to fix it. This remedial work is carried out by a sort of group instinct; not one-to-one, patient to therapist, as on Sigmund Freud's psycho-analytical couch. It's done automatically by real-life group feedback. And group feedback, as we all know, is an unstoppable and sometimes painful human device. People gossip and what others around us say can be immensely revealing, but it can also kill.

In his short and fascinating book *Experiences in Groups*, published in 1961, Wilfred Bion introduced group therapy as follows:

> The term 'group therapy' can have two meanings. It can refer to the treatment of a number of individuals assembled for special therapeutic sessions, or it can refer to a planned endeavour to develop in a group the forces that lead to smoothly running cooperative activity.
>
> The therapy of individuals assembled in groups is usually in the nature of explanation of neurotic trouble, with re-assurance; and sometimes it turns mainly on the catharsis of public confession. The therapy of groups is likely to turn on the acquisition of knowledge and experience of the factors which make for a good group spirit.

A group of say eight people sits together and effectively does nothing. The group performs no formal task. But being people, men and women, they quickly say hello and introduce themselves. First impressions are mentally registered. They tell each other who they are, and surprisingly quickly confessional hints begin to appear about the personal difficulties each one thinks they have. They then get down to the serious business of sorting out each other's social weaknesses and failings. Because of our strong social instincts this happens naturally. As they get to know each other it surfaces spontaneously while they talk. Like in the school playground they do it without external leadership, guidance or prompting.

There is a professional expert, present at all times, who observes the group but refuses to take a lead. The expert only steps in to avoid any serious nastiness.

If the group is a therapeutic success, which isn't always guaranteed, the participants sort out each other's social failings and each goes away with a heightened awareness of their own social habits and an idea of how to improve those that cause problems.

This technique has been improved over the years and adapted successfully to a very wide variety of social situations. As Wilfred Bion pointed out, it depends on the natural development in every working group of what he called a 'proto-mind', in other words not a real mind but an 'as if', or quasi-mind. He explained this phenomenon as a matrix of physical and mental causes:

> The proto-mental system I visualise as one in which physical and mental or psychological are undifferentiated. It is a matrix from which spring the phenomena which at first appear – on a psychological level and in the light of psychological investigation – to be discrete; feelings only loosely associated with one another. It is from this matrix that emotions proper to the basic assumption flow to reinforce, pervade, and, on occasion to dominate the mental life of the group.
>
> From *Experiences in Groups*, op.cit., page 102

Being therapists at heart, and keen to preserve their scientific objectivity, one thing Wilfred Bion and his colleagues shied away from was the nature of the will of the group. They did not examine what Nietzsche had called 'the will to power'. Being psychiatrists, they had no need to question it. More specifically they did not ask where it comes from.

Bion did of course recognise the will of the group, examining at least what it does if not where it comes from. For example, on p. 65 of his *Experiences in Groups* he says:

> Group mentality is the unanimous expression of the will of the group, contributed to by the individual in ways of which he is unaware . . . It is thus a machinery of intercommunication that is designed to ensure that group life is in accordance with basic assumptions.

He leaves it at that; the existence of this will is taken for granted. But it cannot be denied that the quasi-mind does possess an internal force of some sort which drives its purpose; something which seems like ambition; almost a life force. The will drives the group's purpose; it is very real; without this corporate thing, whatever it is, there can be no quasi-mind.

I'm going to say more about life force and mortality at the end of The Employee's Tale.

T-Groups at the Avon Rubber Company

In 1965 I was recruited by John Swanborough to join the Avon Rubber Company. I began as financial controller and was soon asked to set up

117

a corporate planning department. John, who had been newly elected as managing director, had a democratic approach to business management. He was impressed by the behavioural theories of the Tavistock Institute. By releasing the creative potential which had been suppressed by military-type autocratic management, these theories promised a much-needed boost to corporate morale.

One of the latest things on the human-resources front, known in those days as the personnel department, was T-Groups. These were being pioneered at Stanford University in the USA. It was thought that the group therapy being developed on both sides of the Atlantic by Bion and others could be extremely useful in business. The idea was that a small team of senior business managers assemble in a hotel room for five or six days with a professional observer, but no agenda, so as to iron each other out in the way I've just described.

Intrigued by these new ideas John Swanborough got together with the Tavistock Institute to organise a T-Group for four of us at Avon Rubber. These were John himself, Peter Fisher, general manager, Bert Kaiser, polymer scientist, and me, financial controller. Senior executives from two other big British companies joined us. All three companies were included in the annual *Times* list of the hundred biggest British companies. Avon was the smallest of the three.

It certainly was an intense experience and though we have all gone our separate ways since then, the bonds created between us were so strong that I would have dropped everything to help any of the others if I had known them to be in serious trouble. There have been a few others on that bonded list, but not many.

We were told that it was the very first T-Group ever to be held in the British Isles. The Tavistock Institute observed us as guinea-pigs.

They sent along Eric Trist, their managing director. Fred Emory put in an appearance, also Gurth Higgins, Harold Bridger and Richard Drake. Later many different variants were developed and structural rules about avoiding psychological damage were introduced. But none of these were used in the event Tavistock put on for us.

The going gradually became tricky as each one of us – and there were eleven in all – soon realised that if we weren't honest with each other and weren't prepared to admit to our social weaknesses we would be picked on. By some inevitable social imperative, self-disclosure and openness ruled the sessions.

The observers from Tavistock only broke their silence when our discussions got bogged down in technicalities; but never to steer us away from being nasty to each other. I vividly remember the episode when one of us, a professional personnel manager, became all technical about his job back at work. Eric Trist broke in with, 'You know, when I hear you talking and I watch your lips moving, you remind me of my mother.' There was a stunned silence. The group then sheepishly got back to the real business of delicately attending to each other's weaknesses.

A Nasty Episode

It was not long after this that another participant, a talented rugby player who had clearly had a brave military background but was a bit of a show-off, almost broke down. He admitted that he sometimes woke in the middle of the night dreaming that he had strangled his lovely young wife, lying in bed beside him. We all froze, realising that we'd gone too far. Whether the confession later benefited the poor chap I don't know, but we went easy on him after that.

Modelling

In the 1970s business modelling swept into management theory. It was a powerful idea which helped financial controllers to promote the use of financial statements to predict alternative future outcomes.

We often use a model to try out alternative decisions before we start a job. Road maps are models in this sense, so are wind tunnels which simulate the performances of aeroplanes, and also architect's drawings. Financial statements are similar. Profit and loss accounts, balance sheets and cash flow statements have already been mentioned above in The Apprentice's Tale. They have been developed over several centuries of double-entry bookkeeping. They are used retrospectively, to show how money has flowed through a business during the past year; where it came from and what it was spent on. But a financial statement can also be used as a model to look forward; to simulate the future outcomes of alternative business decisions. In a way this is a bit like playing computer games.

Money flows in from sales and flows out to pay for resources. Predicting the different components, as in a river basin, of the in-and-out flowing of money is a highly effective way of understanding how a company *performs*. Especially if, rather than being mesmerised by the bank notes, one thinks instead about the labour, raw materials and equipment these are being traded for. In fact, that's the very thing this book examines: how do the wheels of a labour-divided, purposeful social unit actually work?

The treasury model of an economy is a brilliant device for planning national tax, savings and investment policies to boost monetary wealth. But there's definitely something missing there. Life can be deadly predictable and boring in a prosperous nation, but good fun and exciting, even amongst the poor, in a poorer one. There seem to be at least two good reasons for this. First, that *Gemeinschaft* units: families, villages and so on, are not suitable for monetisation. And second, that we can't measure happiness, misery or emotion. The ideas put forward in PART 2 below claim to show how by using A&PT it might be possible to bring the psychological dimension into the management of our social lives.

Business Modelling

Business modelling is like playing computer games. The difference is that instead of competing, military-style, in a landscape, participants are running an imaginary business whose financial situation mirrors their own real-life company. Business games are like sophisticated versions of the famous board game *Monopoly*.

The purpose of business modelling is to enable senior executives to make back-of-the-envelope reviews of the possible outcomes of different pricing, employment and capital-investment policies and combinations of these. The objective is not maximising cash flow or profit, it is beating the competition: maximising market share. Cash is a limiting factor. Fast moving autocratic entrepreneurs might keep these workings closely secret; more democratic corporate bosses might choose to display and discuss them with their management teams.

Strategically the balance is between two mutually exclusive extremes: squeezing maximum cash out of the business or going all-out to grab a bigger share of the market. These ideas were promoted worldwide with great success by Bruce Henderson and his Boston

Consulting group. He came to visit us at BOC.

These new management techniques powerfully harnessed corporate ambition, also known as corporate greed. They were quickly noticed by politicians and they gave an intellectual boost to the wave of privatisations spearheaded somewhat clumsily in the 1980s by Margaret Thatcher and Ronald Reagan.

Business Games at BOC

At British Oxygen (BOC) in the 1970s I devised a simple business game which was used at our management training centre at Chartridge, near Amersham, where a wide variety of lectures, demonstrations and corporate social events took place during long weekends. We called it The Controller's Game; senior executives from our various subsidiaries – engineers, marketing managers and accountants – competed in teams. Like card games it was played in rounds, and like bridge, the game had a risk-taking element. The purpose was to illustrate the interplay between the different decisions a company, large or small, must make every day.

Apart from the use of modelling as a financial training aid and a valuable exercise in team building, we aimed to send executives back to their day-jobs with the knowledge needed to apply these ideas at work. Crucially also these exercises showed us all how a conglomerate should function: its mechanisms. These simple training exercises enabled us to illustrate the interrelated workings of a hierarchy of inter-penetrating but fiercely independent social units. It was easy to see how the size advantages of belonging to a large conglomerate were shared out among our subsidiaries so as to increase the group's shares of the interconnected markets we were in. The general idea was that people who understand how and why strategic decisions are being taken are better motivated to execute them than those who are kept in the dark.

Sadly, before this democratising device had a chance to blossom, a management upheaval broke out in the BOC parent company. Using the slogan: FORGET ABOUT DISCOUNTED CASH FLOW: IT'S THE BOTTOM LINE, STUPID, a new faction swept in. Like a wrecking ball, it smashed through and swept away the training centre, and much else besides, including me and the rest of the top management of BOC Ltd.

About five years later this new regime blundered big-time and BOC took a long nosedive. Inevitably its ownership and management were eventually taken over by our German rivals. These were the Thatcher years, and though this saga was typical of the time, it's still a painful memory.

How the Game Works

Let us assume your company wants to succeed in beating the competition, not in a terrific hurry but to get the upper hand by taking better decisions than them, methodically, over a period of years.

There really are only five sets of decisions which are incorporated in every business strategy. These are the ones that link the present with the future, and which affect all the functions of the business. They must be combined. None can be taken in isolation.

In a small company, one person, the boss, takes all these decisions alone, intuitively balancing one against the other. It's only when the business gets too big for this that the tasks begin to be delegated among different people. Intuition, or 'gut-feel', has to be assisted by formal teamwork.

The five decisions a manufacturer has to take are:

How many will we make?

What price will we charge?

How much will we spend on marketing?

How much should we spend on production capacity?

How much should we spend on research?

Labour supply is not really a strategic decision; it is not part of this interconnected set of five. Like electricity supply or managerial quality, it is more like a resource optimisation problem.

These five gaming decisions are obviously interconnected. The price you propose to charge affects the quantity you make. The quantity you make depends on the production capacity you invest in, and that in turn affects the price you charge. And so on.

The management team must understand the way, formal or in-stinctive, autocratic or democratic, these internally consistent decisions are made. It's a long game repeated year after year.

The next thing is the 'expand–fund' balancing act. The name of the game here is to assess the skill and the aggression of your rivals, and then to aim to expand faster and yet be able to fund that expansion. It's a delicate balance which has to take international market forces into account. The big spender expands too fast and goes broke, but the miser goes too slowly and is overtaken. So, the five strategic decisions don't simply have to be consistent with each other, they have to be either consistently expansionary or consistently cautious. The balance between the two is the most crucial management task, and it applies to the small street-market trader and the gigantic car manufacturer alike.

The long game is always competition – be too cautious and you'll lose out, too fast and you'll go broke. The limiting factor is always cash flow.

The five decision sets in this simple but universal business game can be adjusted to suit any particular business. Some enterprises like Oxygen production are capital intensive, others like a chain of restaurants are marketing intensive. Each will have a slightly different balance of criteria which is vital for success.

The Rounds of Business Game Play and Adjudication

One day is usually needed to play the game. Each round of play takes about an hour. Each round represents six months of real-life trading. Four or five teams of four players take part.

After explaining the rules, the adjudicator starts the game by handing a notional lump sum of cash and a factory to each team. They then have thirty minutes to make their trading and investment decisions.

Selling price decisions come in high, medium and low. More factory units can be bought from the adjudicator, but there's a delay of six months, one round, before these come on stream. There is only one product. Marketing effort and research can be bought. There is no borrowing, and no debtors or creditors are left on the books at the end of a round. Inventories of unsold products are carried over to the following round. The adjudicators can increase the tempo by arbitrarily changing the overall size of the market to simulate fluctuations in consumer demand, seasonal factors and so on.

At the end of each round the adjudicating team uses random tables or a computer to work out the results of each team's trading decisions.

At the start of each new round the adjudicator hands these results to each team. The results come with a skeleton profit and loss account and balance sheet. These are published to everybody.

Each round represents six months of real life. The basic tasks each team performs every round are: 1. reviewing, 2. planning and 3. decision making. (In PART 2 below these tasks are described as The Rule of Three).

Adjudication can be intense. We used combinations of pocket calculators, random tables and the rolling of dice. Those were the days before personal computers and, though tailor-made programmes would have speeded it all up and made it more sophisticated, such games can be played entirely 'by hand' without losing the essentials.

The game then proceeds by successive rounds of play until the day is over. The team with the highest sales in the final round is declared the winner. Time for adjudicator's impressions and general discussion is allowed for at the end.

Actually, when we played the game some teams went bankrupt while others were clearly the most successful. Usually it was easy for the adjudicator to declare a winner by reviewing the market share, the cash situation and the plant and equipment, in other words by looking at the profit and loss account and balance sheet of each team. By the end of the day, all participants – winners, bankrupts and adjudicators – had had rich experiences and resolutions to take back to their day jobs.

Gaming showed me how to identify and examine the inter-connected working mechanisms, the machinery, of a monetised social unit. The proof that these techniques are universally applicable to all monetised groups, *Gesellschafts*, fuelled my belief that it must surely be possible to do the same for all social groups, including non-monetised *gemeinschafts*. The answers would have to accommodate social electricity, more commonly called emotion. This belief became my Holy Grail, it is what has kept me going through research setbacks and academic rejections. The assembly and performance thinking outlined in PART 2 is the best I have been able to come up with.

What's Life All About?

It wasn't a concern to the child, the student, apprentice or mother, but the employee does begin to wonder: What's the point of it all? Doubts and questions begin to creep in. Some call it the mid-life crisis. 'What's life all about, have I wasted it?' 'Should I be putting something back into the community?' 'Is life actually about anything at all?'

'Life's Like A Banana.' I once saw that scribbled in English on the lavatory wall of the Brasserie de l'Isle Saint-Louis, our favourite pub in Paris. It could well be a quote from Dante, Chaucer or Boccaccio. The full version goes: 'Life's like a banana, one minute it's in yer hand; the next it's up yer arse.'

Well actually, life's not at all like a banana; it's more like a video game. (This point is made below under video games in The Senior Citizen's Tale). Indeed, why should life be about anything at all? It does seem to be a homocentric question; fuelled by hubris. Let's try to turn it inside out.

We can say that dead things are not alive. A blade of grass, for example. One minute it's stiff, green and healthy looking, the next it isn't. It's limp, lifeless and dead. Something has vanished. What was that? What was it that has vanished? One answer is that life is what's vanished. So, at the very least, we can say that life is a 'thing' which vanishes on death.

Now this thing, whatever it is, that vanishes on death, is central in all major religions; they call it 'the soul'. As soon as they do that, they float off into Plato's fantasy world. They go into fantasies about God in heaven, the everlasting life up there if you're good, and eternal damnation if you're not. These crazy ideas can make it difficult to think about the fundamental nature of life.

Even scientists seem reluctant to admit in public that if they want to create life, they must endow inert matter with will or ambition; with this thing, whatever it is, that inert matter lacks.

The Essence of Life: the will to metabolise, self-protect and breed

As Mark Haw at the University of Strathclyde, and others, have pointed out, the essential life functions boil down to three interconnected sets: metabolising (i.e., acquiring energy), self-protection and reproducing. One on its own is not enough; all three must be present, one way or another, in every life form. And the clincher is that all three must be governed, orchestrated, driven, motivated, by a will. To repeat: will, or ambition is the 'thing' which the scientist who wants to create life, must bestow in inert matter.

The central argument in the assembly and performance thinking promoted in PART 2 is that this will exists in the quasi-minds of cooperating groups just as it does in those of individual creatures.

But the will of the group does not exist in the mind of any one individual: not even in the leaders. As quoted above, Wilfred Bion said it only exists in 'as-if' form in the matrix or proto-mind of the group. Similar observations have been made by many other people including Bernard Mandeville, J. J. Rousseau and Gustave Le Bon.

Society Is All Too Complicated

But the employee just gets on with the job and doesn't really want to bother with all that psychological sociology stuff. It's a disputed field and the experts often find it difficult to get their ideas across. For example, J. H. Turner, a highly respected and much cited American sociologist, writes about how society works in Chapter 2 of *Handbook of Contemporary Sociological Theory*, published in 2016. The chapter is called 'Integrating and Disintegrating Dynamics in Human Societies'. On page 19 he defines *integration* as:

> Simply the modes and mechanisms by which social units and the social activities in and between them are coordinated into coherent patterns of social organisation and the potential of these mechanisms to stave off, or to accelerate the inevitable disintegration of all patterns of social organisation.

Turner goes on to say, also on page19:

> As I will argue, integration and disintegration operate at all
> three levels of human social organization: (1) the micro universe
> of integration in face-to-face encounters, (2) the meso world of
> [a] corporate units (groups organizations and communities)
> revealing divisions of labor and [b] categoric units built from
> social distinctions based on criteria such as ethnicity, religion,
> gender, and age that become bases for moral evaluation of
> members of subpopulations in a society, and (3) the macro
> systems of (a) institutional domains and (b) stratification
> systems as these become the pillars of (c) societal and (d) inter-
> societal systems.

Turner then ends Chapter 2 as follows:

> At the very least, I have proposed that integration is a multi-
> level and complex process that cannot be theorized at any one
> level of social organization. We cannot simply pronounce
> processes – say integration rituals, self-verification, exchange,
> cultural fields, networks, etc. – as a master mechanism of
> societal integration. This has been the theoretical tendency, and
> it has led scholars to abandon the effort to develop a general
> theory of integration. But once we seek integration as a series of
> mechanisms operating at distinct levels of social reality, and
> then, across levels of reality, we place ourselves in a position to
> develop a more robust theory.

The question was roughly: How do groups combine to form a society? In view of such a daunting explanation by J. H. Turner, a distinguished professor of sociology, it's not surprising that the politician prefers to leave it all to the academics until the academics can teach us how to interpret their scholarly insights into everyday politics. Unfortunately, they cannot do that yet.

Social Electricity: Emotion Cannot Be Measured

Tantalisingly, financial statements cannot account for, or measure, social electricity. Social excitement jazzes up morale, peer pressure, harmony, happiness, emotion, *esprit de corps*, hysteria, anger, fear, panic, and so on. Social electricity is what makes the whole thing tick. When the chips are down the irrational trumps the rational. Social electricity is what assembled the social unit – family, tribe or nation – in the very first place; it continually refreshes society. Switch it off and society collapses like an empty glove puppet. Emotion is described in PART 2 as an essential social safety-valve. I will claim that this insight validates assembly and performance thinking.

The Soul and Measuring Happiness Are Still Out of Reach

The employee on holiday has just settled down with a really good novel. But suddenly two stray dogs start a vicious fight and a storm of emotion upsets his equilibrium. Emotion sweeps calm rationality aside and when it's over the old doubts about problems back at work, how to measure happiness, and questions about mortality and the soul come flapping back like recently disturbed crows. But eventually, unless he is actually paid for thinking about reality, the employee settles back to read his book.

> And it was said indeed by many a man
> That never since the day the world began
> In all God's earth, wide seas and reach of land,
> Had so few men made such a noble band
> As in respect of knighthood and degree.
> Everyone with a taste for chivalry
> And keen (you bet) to win a glorious name
> Had begged to be allowed to join the game.

From *The Knight's Tale*, Geoffrey Chaucer

THE SENIOR CITIZEN'S TALE

Seniors Come Last

We seniors are the last to tell our tale, so we are the only ones who have listened to everybody else. We have loved the child's fresh simplicity, smiled at the student's brash confidence, winced at the memory of all those exams the apprentice had to sit, marvelled at the modest resilience of the mother, and we have noticed the competitive nature of the worker.

But the senior is still not clear about how society actually works. Who got it right? Was it the left-wing idealistic student or the weather-beaten, experienced, right-wing employee? And if society is amenable to science why can't sociologists explain it to us? There are always more questions than answers.

Social Collapse and Regeneration: The French Revolution, etc.

Senior citizens have watched many episodes of social collapse. We have read about the Reign of Terror in France after the French Revolution and about Spain during the Inquisition. The destructive behaviour of Nazi Germany and Communist Russia are still in living memory. We have witnessed the anarchy of popular rebellions in Northern Ireland and South Africa. On TV we see Islamic fundamentalists destroying their own communities in the Middle East. We have watched world-leading corporations in the British steel and chemical industries being swept aside by lower-wage-paying foreign competitors. These all illustrate the misery and pain of social breakdown.

Witch-hunts can kill but they also purge, and good sometimes comes out of social collapse. A sort of witch-hunt is going on right now at the start of the twenty-first century in the British Isles. It is against men who make unwelcome sexual advances towards women. Good will surely come of it. Women are at last empowered to wag the finger at the oafish boss. Even the most powerful men now understand that they must respect the other person's point of view and behave properly. Without this witch-hunt nothing would have changed.

The Tale of Two Cities by Charles Dickens ends with the heroic death of Sydney Carton during the Terror in Paris. It was a fearful episode when the innocent often were falsely denounced by the mob and guillotined. Shocking? Yes! We believe we are much too civilised today for such barbarism. But are we really? How does it all work?

Introduction to Social Tangles, Emergence and Social Energy

Georg Hegel and Karl Marx both wrote convincingly about the 'dialectical' way in which social movements seem to swing between opposite tendencies, for example from capitalism to socialism and back again. We seniors have lived long enough to notice this happening. Charismatic orators tend to keep reinventing the wheel. The brilliant speeches delivered in the eighteenth century by the great Irish orator Edmund Burke to the British parliament could be spoken again almost word-for-word in the House of Commons today. The fashions in women's clothing which were all the rage fifty years ago keep resurfacing, and the same old pub jokes come around at twenty-five-year intervals. 'What goes around comes around,' or, as they say in France, 'Plus ça change, plus c'est la même chose.'

The dialectic offers a sweeping history of society, but it doesn't tell us about its daily workings. It can explain what has happened but cannot predict when the pendulum will reverse itself. The Child's Tale saw society as so tangled in inconsistencies and three-dimensional knots of family, money and law, that there seemed no hope of ever understanding it.

But then regular patterns of social behaviour gradually begin to appear. So, the idea of 'emergence' as a phenomenon; a thing which we can examine in its own right becomes a possible answer. Furthermore it seems possible that if these regularities could somehow be socially animated with the hot breath of emotion, like laying today's weather forecast over the tide tables to forecast the sea-state, then we might get a bit further in the quest to understand how society works. So, to the senior questing for the reality of social mechanisms there seem to be three things which become apparent one after the other: 1. Social tangles, 2. Emergence and 3. Social energy.

1. Social tangles and chaos

Chaos is the name we give to a process we notice but don't understand, it's a bit like lumbago. We can remember how in the 1950s when we went to the doctor with a pain in the lower back, he'd examine you carefully and then say you had lumbago. That made you feel better until you looked it up in a dictionary which said lumbago is 'rheumatic pain in the lower muscles of the back.'

The Shorter Oxford Dictionary says the scientific meaning of chaos is: 'behaviour of a system which is governed by deterministic laws but is so unpredictable as to appear random, owing to its extreme sensitivity to initial conditions'. That just about sums up society from the child's point of view: it looks like chaos. But when we watch this apparent chaos with great patience, regular patterns do seem to emerge.

2. Emergence exemplified by *Robert's Rules*

Emergence is the name we give to regularly recurring patterns which we do not fully understand, and so cannot predict. Examples include earthquakes and traffic systems. Emergence is what happens when a working system responds successfully to a stimulus and the thing that emerges was not inherent in its stimulants. One of the conditions which can make things emerge is synergy; this is the rather marvellous happening in which an outcome is greater than the sum of its parts.

Holistic Darwinism (2005) by Peter A. Corning was one of the first, and is still one of the best books, I have come across while researching the mechanisms of society. Corning defines synergy on page 50 as follows:

> . . . synergy is a ubiquitous and fundamentally important aspect of the natural world . . . Synergy, broadly defined, refers to combined or cooperative effects – literally, the effects produced

by things that operate together (parts, elements or individuals). The term is frequently associated with the slogan 'the whole is greater than the sum of its parts' (which traces back to Aristotle in the *Metaphysics*) or '2 + 2 = 5', but as we shall see, this is actually a caricature, a narrow and perhaps even misleading definition of a multifaceted concept. I prefer to say that the effects produced by wholes are *different* from what the parts can produce separately.

Emergence is a description of what happens rather than why it happens. Examples in the physical world include hurricanes and snowflakes. In the living world, behaviours we observe but can't fully explain include ant-nest ventilation systems, termite 'cities' and human societies. We say they just 'emerge'. Alternative results are subject to natural selection and when the most useful outcomes are used repeatedly, they are said to 'emerge'.

Committee work is a good example. In committee work participants come together at regular intervals. As a group they consider progress since their last meeting, discuss what needs to be done, and plan how to do it. There is someone, a chairman, who keeps order, and someone else, a secretary, who records what has been agreed. In one form or another whenever a group of any size assembles at regular intervals to get things done, these same functions emerge. It will have happened in ancient Egypt and happens all over the world today. This is the efficient way for groups to get things done. The very fact that a group has assembled presupposes internal democracy. The only alternative is autocracy, but this stifles the creative power of a group.

The enduring use of *Robert's Rules of Order* illustrates emergence; this is a reference book like the *FA Handbook*. *Robert's Rules* was written in 1876 by H. M. Robert, an American army officer; it has been republished eleven times and has so far sold six million copies. The book is not based on military procedures. It is offered for use by a wide range of groups from the smallest parent-teacher associations to parliaments. Here's how the purpose of the book is explained on page iii of the 2011 edition:

> Generally, *Robert's Rules of Order* is a guide for conducting meetings and making decisions as a group. The purpose of the book is to enable assemblies of any size, with due regard for every member's opinion, to arrive at the general will on the maximum number of questions of varying complexity in a minimum amount of time and under all kinds of internal climate ranging from total harmony to hardened or impassioned division of opinion.

This book is an excellent description of how every human group must proceed after it has *assembled*. It illustrates the working mechanisms of human group *performance*.

The prior process of assembly is quite separate and is not considered in these rules. This confirms the distinction between assembly and performance which is central in PART 2 below.

3. Social energy is like water pressure

The observation that these regular patterns of cooperative behaviour keep re-emerging helps to clarify our thoughts about how society works. Emergence-thinking is all very logical, very rational, but it doesn't take the emotions, the fluctuations of excitement, or social energy, into account. It does not deal with the irrational. The power of emotion has already been mentioned briefly in The Employee's Tale.

The senior wonders how society works. He or she realises that any answers which cannot account for the irrational, which only apply when things are normal, merely answer half the question. After all, crises, panics and excitements are happening all the time, and even when they are not, the newspapers, radio and TV do their best to persuade us that they are.

Even when there is no external threat, the dialectical pendulum of society swings back and forth – for example, between austerity and profligacy, autocracy and democracy. When it has swung too far one way an extra effort is usually injected, often dosed with emotion, to stop its momentum and re-stabilise the system by getting it to swing back the other way again. This emotional re-stabilising tendency is another form of emergence.

At home, water comes out of the tap in two simultaneous states: pressure and volume, and the same is roughly true of social energy. Water-pressure is determined by the height of the water-column whereas the amount or volume of water coming out depends on how much the tap is opened. If we open the tap very slightly out comes a small stream, whereas a very wide opening sends out a sudden gush.

Social energy is similar in that two states can be distinguished.

It's clear that somehow groups have the ability to adjust the impact of this two-state energy when responding to an external threat. This adjustment is orchestrated by a group consensus or quasi-mind.

Given a fixed number of members the group can use emotion to adjust the impact, or *volume*, of their response to a disturbance. A few soldiers acting suddenly and fiercely together can alter a battle. But though it may be potentially violent, emotion soon blows over; *the header tank is quickly emptied*. The answer is that volume of a group's energy depends on its size, so to increase the volume element of its response, the group must recruit more talent or assemble more members; the army must increase its quality or size.

When the potential of a group – a football team or a chain of restaurants – is in question both these factors have to be considered. To increase its overall pressure the group must somehow take on new recruits, increase the height of the water-column, whereas to increase its impact, temporarily and within the limits of its overall power, it must open the 'volume-tap'.

Furthermore, these two factors, power and impact, are constantly constraining and revitalising each other. The better the group performs the easier it becomes to find new recruits, and vice versa. In PART 2 below it is suggested that to understand the dynamics of this vice-versa interplay, it is necessary to separate the *assembly* of a group (the raising of its water-column) from its *performance* (the opening up of its volume-tap).

Video Games Deliver Group Savvy Youngsters off the Conveyor Belt

FIFA is the name of a video game in which game-players do the manager's job as well as acting as the footballers. The winner is the one whose team tops the league. In this game the same problem, the vice-versa 'constraint and revitalisation challenge', is central.

Baseball is a similar video game, but my favourite is *Hitwicketcricket.com* because of the way in which sudden death, out in the sun, is simulated. When a goal is scored the play resumes, but when the ball hits the batsman's stumps that's it. Click! He's dead. In these games the manager, alias for the teenage gamer, starts with a huge lottery win, buys a team of players in the Indian Premier League and sends them out to bat and then to field. Chance is built into outcomes, and risks are taken. Success or failure on the field then feeds back to team selection by increasing or reducing the manager's available funds.

In *Robert's Rules of Order*, (mentioned under Emergence above), we already noticed the difference between assembly and performance, and here it is again in team-manager video games. These games are enormously popular. In June 2018, the World Health Organisation included 'gaming disorder' in its International Classification of Diseases in recognition of the growing worldwide addiction of youngsters to these games. The addictive quality of these games can surely only be explained by the way they simulate the *assemblies and performances* of real life.

We senior citizens are perplexed as we watch our grandchildren playing video games. In round after round the various challenges of real life are simulated. Some games are more realistic than others, and as always, some youngsters are more easily addicted than others. What effect these vivid mental experiences will have on future generations we can't predict. It may be little but at least they will have excellent keyboard skills.

To the observer, these games seem, like a conveyor belt, to be spilling successive waves of computer savvy youngsters into society. The latest generation will soon be adults, so it's possible that many of them will already have been primed to accept as plainly obvious the distinction between getting a group together and how it then performs. In other words this new generation may already have learnt from *FIFA*, *Baseball Manager*, and *Hitwicketcricket* how groups play their internal 'vice-versa' feedback skills, and how they then interact with other groups in the slow-motion maelstrom of real life which we call society.

(Video gaming is further discussed in PART 3 below under *Video-gaming addiction*).

There's Something Greedy about Philosophy

And another thing many of us seniors have spotted. From the senior's perspective there seems to be something greedy about philosophy. It deals exclusively in the imponderables of life. As soon as science explains a mystery, the atomic periodic table for example, philosophy quietly sneaks off the stage. It specialises in things we don't understand and probably never will: things like infinity, existence, consciousness and knowledge. By this means the great philosophers like Plato, Descartes, Kant, Wittgenstein and Derrida seem able to grab the intellectual high ground with effortless ease. But we all learnt at school to make sure we'd got our facts right before we put our hand up; it was a lesson in humility. In her tale the mother has already dismissed Plato's cosmology as pure hubris and the senior citizen has seen enough of life to detect something pushy, shrill, greedy even, about philosophy; it seems to put its hand up before understanding the basics.

Philosophy draws attention to itself, confident that it has the best methods to answer most problems. There is a philosophy of science but there isn't a science of philosophy; Bertrand Russell thought he had found one in mathematical logic, but his pupil Wittgenstein showed it to be inadequate. There seem to be echoes here of the way Aristotle, the pupil, brought his great master Plato down to earth.

Philosophy examines existence from a personal, human, point of view. It is essentially the 'I' who am asking the questions. It deals with eternally fascinating questions about reality, knowledge, existence, time, the soul and consciousness. No harm in that so far as it goes, but then it overreaches when it claims to explain social life: the life of the 'we'; of 'us', before understanding the social basics like natural selection, emotion and the mechanisms of group behaviour. The better attitude here would be to recognise that questions about how society works are beyond the scope of philosophy.

We seniors recognise with awe that the great encyclopaedia of human knowledge is getting bigger every day, and every profession is becoming more and more specialised. The stars on a clear night twinkle out there in deep space. The light we see is billions of years old. We wonder: OK, so what's happening out there right now; at this moment? We're told that we really only know what happened recently to any but a few of the closest stars. For the rest, the light emitted by what's happening out there right now won't reach us for a very long time, so we simply don't know. For all we know they might already have vanished.

It's the same with the very tiniest things. Apparently atoms, which were proposed by Democritus, active around 400BC and other ancient Greeks, are absolutely enormous in comparison to the very smallest things we 'know' about: things like quarks, gluons and waves which we believe must be in there, or should that be 'down' there? And beneath those smallest 'things' there probably exist still smaller ones. And even if there is nothing smaller than those quarks and gluons, we must still remember that they are said to be the basis of everything. So how do they interact to construct the land we live on, and to produce the very thoughts we have? The more we learn during our long lives, the greater becomes the size of our ignorance. But the excitement of discovery is so addictive, even to us senior citizens, that our curiosity is never diminished.

> What minstrelsy, what service at the feast
> How richly decked the palace, what the place
> Ordained at first and last upon the dais,
> What ladies loveliest in the dancing throng
> And which most exquisite in dance and song
> And which to speak most feelingly of love,
> Or what the falcons that were perched above,
> And what the hounds that crouched upon the floor –
> Of all such questions I shall say no more
> Than the result of it: I will not tease you,
> Here comes the point, so listen if it please you.

From *The Knight's Tale*, Geoffrey Chaucer

PART 2

SOCIAL THEORY ASSEMBLY

ASSEMBLY

PART 1 showed that the mechanisms of society are visible everywhere we look; we are all immersed in it. All of us: infant, criminal, parent, farmer, archbishop and prime minister, we all rely on society for all our individual needs to take on energy, protect ourselves and to breed. The main argument in PART 2 is that the way to understand how society works is to distinguish between the assembly of working groups and the way they perform their work.

The Child's Tale showed that the only ways we can experience society are through sight, hearing, touch, taste and smell; nobody can get first-hand social experience from anywhere else. Everything we pick up from friends, books, teachers, TV, radio, newspapers and so on, is second hand. That may be obvious, but it is a way of reminding ourselves how closely we rely on each other. It also helps us to think twice about dubious things, like God and human self-importance, which come to us second hand: through culture. These are the thoughts of others. The workings of culture are a key feature of assembly.

The Dilemma of Assembly

The assembly of a working group is an extremely difficult achievement in evolutionary biology. It should on the face of it have been impossible for nature to evolve a cooperating creature. This is because genetically endowed natural selfishness is a necessary condition for evolution by natural selection. So, before individuals can be recruited into working groups this selfishness must be suppressed in favour of altruism. Scholars differ on some of the details, but the generally accepted solution to this dilemma, first proposed by Pyotr Kropotkin and indeed by Darwin himself, is that natural selfishness can be side-stepped if the breeding group rather than the individual can become the unit of selection. In such an arrangement it is the 'fittest' group that is naturally selected rather than the 'fittest' individual.

The Tramlines of Culture

Culture develops naturally in all cooperating mammals. It can be thought of as well trodden paths or tramlines which enable newly invented useful ideas and behaviours to pass from one individual to another and on down from one generation to the next. It is a powerful force which coordinates and regulates our social lives. It is even suggested that because of our ability to read and write, cultural adaptation in humans is partially replacing the much slower processes of natural selection. This may explain why *Homo sapiens* is no longer spinning off sub-species in the way that butterflies do, for example, or orchids and wasps. In this view it is culture rather than speciation[1] which enables us to adapt; we can harness technology in order to thrive in special situations; mountainous, tropical or arctic, all over the globe. We have even used technology to metabolise and self-protect ourselves on the moon, albeit briefly. This 'adaptation by culture' process may help to explain what one could call 'reverse speciation', in which sub-species

1 The formation of new and distinct species in the course of evolution.

such as Neanderthals and Denisovans are believed to have been absorbed backwards into a broad animal species now called *Homo sapiens*.

The writing of marks to convey sounds was first developed about five thousand years ago. It appears to have been achieved independently in several isolated parts of the world at about the same time. The story is beautifully told in *Writing: Making your Mark*, published in 2019 by the British Library, edited by Ewan Clayton. Writing may be a mighty powerful cultural tool, but that doesn't prevent it from leading us astray. From the very beginning it seems to have been a powerful factor in building the religious myth that mankind is unique in the universe; even the very purpose for which it was created in the first place. This seductive story is told in all the world's major religions. I was brought up on the Christian Bible which begins with: 'So God created mankind in his own image, in the image of God he created them; male and female he created them' (from the New International Version, Genesis 1.27). This glorious cosmology helps to explain why mankind, with a few nasty exceptions, is so intelligent, beautiful and benevolent.

To this day and, despite the fact this is obvious nonsense, I still can't get myself to spell God with a lower-case 'g'. That is a nice demonstration of the visceral power of culture. Culture has enhanced the survival and prosperity of *Homo sapiens* in numerous ways. Among these is the massive fallacy which I think of as the mound of Platonic detritus called hubris. It is still deeply embedded in our cultures; particularly in the assumptions underpinning classical philosophy, also in economics and in sociology. I'm saying here that it has to be side-stepped if we are to understand how society works.

I suggested repeatedly in PART 1 that hubris prevents straight thinking about how society really works. I will begin PART 2 with a description of the mechanisms of ASSEMBLY. I will try to show that if we can side-step the hubristic fallacy, not easy to do because it is so deeply embedded in our culture, then a veritable cascade of perceptions about how assembly is achieved can tumble forth. These come next; they are spiced with humility about *Homo sapiens* and with a sense of how little we seem to know about the mechanisms of society. There are fourteen interconnected thoughts in this cascade. Some of them have been evolved over millions of generations dating back well before our ancient ape ancestors. They may be stitched together in an unusual way here, but not one is original; they all rely on existing scholarship. There is, inevitably, some repetition in this cascade of mechanisms because they are so interconnected.

Like a barrister's portfolio of his best arguments, these fourteen explanations are a mixture of scene setting and killer points. When taken together, they hope to explain how human individuals are able to ASSEMBLE into cohesive work-performing units, in spite of natural selfishness.

If the argument that group assembly is a distinct and biologically difficult achievement and is one which is quite distinct from group performance, can be falsified, then my assembly and performance thinking collapses like a pack of cards.

1. AMBITION IS THE UNSOLVED ESSENCE OF LIFE

The recognition that the groups we form have quasi-minds (see the Employee's Tale above, also *Groups Acquire Quasi-minds* below) presents a series of regressive, Russian-doll type, questions; each answer reveals yet another deeper question.

1. The first question is: what motivates this group quasi-mind?
    Answer: our individual ambitions: we each want to survive
    and prosper.

2. OK then, next question: why assemble at all? Answer: because
    together we enhance our chances.

3. Next: so how does a group do that for me? Answer: either by
    helping me to eat better, be safer, or to raise children better
    than I could if I were a solitary creature.

4. Yes, but: why do I even want to survive and prosper? Answer:
    because being alive means I have somehow been endowed
    with this ambition.

5. So, this smallest doll sends me right back to 1: to the
    unexplained essence of life, and nobody can yet say how life
    is endowed with ambition.

We do not know how will or ambition is endowed on inert matter.
We can understand how we might be able to make the necessary
components: the DNA blueprints, chemical circuits, cell-parts, molecular motors, and metabolism systems. But we do not understand how
to give them ambition or will. If we could do that it would mean that
we could create life. As humans we all *want* to survive and prosper,

accordingly our ancestors evolved the ability to cooperate, and this has greatly improved our chances. That's why we conform to society, but it doesn't explain why we actually *wanted* to survive and prosper in the first place. We cannot endow ambition; we are not as clever as we often think.

2. A WEEDING DEFINITION OF EVOLUTION

The process of evolution shows that humans are just animals. This undermines our sense of self-importance: our hubris. It brings us down to earth. So, it's not surprising that controversy still surrounds our acceptance of evolution by natural selection. Deep in our literary heritage and at the roots of our religions and folklores and in our children's fairy tales, we still cling to the fallacy that humans must be the centre point, and even the whole purpose of nature. Reality doesn't sell nearly so well as self-congratulatory fiction.

Evolution by natural selection is not a provable fact, indeed it's not a fact at all; it's a process. It's an amazing process which emerges immediately life is created. It is the result of the opposition between ambition and attrition. All life forms are endowed with the will, the ambition, to metabolise, self-protect and breed. This then triggers behaviour which is opposed both by other life forms and by inert dangers: temperatures, pressures, gases, and so on. So here we have individuals motivated by internal ambitions and opposed by external agents. The result is that the least well-endowed are weeded out and fail to reproduce. By this weeding process life can diversify into myriad forms to exploit myriad niches in its ambitious pursuit of metabolism, self-protection and breeding. Apologies for the repetition here but this m, s-p & b triumvirate of imperatives, which together make up ambition, is important.

One of these myriad niches is cooperation. If a creature can work with others the better to metabolise, self-protect or breed, and especially all three, it thereby gets an advantage over those that cannot. Cooperation is thus a niche available to all life forms, including plants and fungi, but it is massively opposed by natural selfishness. The various ways in which this opposition has been overcome by certain creatures in almost every animal order including humans, are discussed here.

It is interesting to remember, from The Student's Tale in PART 1, that society can sometimes be seen as a collection of individuals, *homo economicus*, and at other times as a hierarchy of groups, *homo reciprocans*, so in passing it may be worth noting that the weeding process of natural selection is likewise understood to operate on both individuals *and* groups. This is quite an important element in assembly and performance thinking; I will be referring to it again below in the 'Spark test'.

3. COOPERATION IS A PRE-EXISTING EVOLUTIONARY NICHE

As with sight, which uses light waves that existed before life began, and hearing, which uses pre-existing sound waves, cooperation despite natural selfishness is another pre-existing evolutionary niche. Here lie opportunities, which occur immediately when life begins, and evolution by natural selection is highly creative when it comes to exploiting opportunity. Like sight and hearing, cooperation has been evolved genetically from the solitary, default condition many times; there is no common cooperating ancestor.

As well as light waves and sound waves, certain life forms also use differential chemical gradients, like taste and smell, to transmit information. Telepathy seems to be a side-track, nevertheless one has to wonder about the several other waves besides light and sound that evidently surround us daily, like microwaves, electric currents, magnetism, radio waves, quantum transmission and gravitational waves. There seems no reason why these could not be used as evolutionary niches by life-forms to get a competitive advantage from the enhanced communication available thereby, perhaps they already are being so used. It's an intriguing thought; light and sound waves, though robustly familiar to us, are by no means the only potential communication channels. Maybe, given a few million years of evolution by natural selection, a species of ant, octopus, naked mole-rat, or even a cooperating species of orchid will, using quantum mechanics, invent telepathy and, using super-assembly, get to rule the world. This is the stuff of science fiction.

4. THE EVOLUTIONARY ORIGIN OF COOPERATION

The quest which John Gibson set me during that bike-ride round Ireland, (see Introduction above) was to find out how natural selection evolved the misuse of human power – so the evolutionary origin of cooperation is a central issue here.

It is sometimes implied that both Hamilton's rule, about altruism in social insects, and game theory, such as the prisoner's dilemma, can explain the evolutionary origin of cooperation. But, (see below, 12. *Hamilton's Rule is Not the Answer*) these arguments take the prior existence of society as given, so they fall into the circular argument trap; they claim to prove that which they have already assumed to be the case.

What is life? We need to answer that before we think about how cooperation may have evolved. Mark Haw (2012) writing in *Nature*, expressed a biologist's view of life as follows: 'Somehow, in living things, matter makes molecular mechanisms with the ability to harvest the energy to organise, maintain and propagate themselves.'

These three life-functions: harvesting energy, maintenance and propagation, are 'survive-and-prosper' motivators. One could loosely call them hunger, fear and sex; they combine to drive evolution by natural selection in living things.

Mark Haw's description probes the nature of life. Why do living things *want to* energise, maintain and propagate themselves at all? This is not just a question of why they do these things; it's why do they even want to do them? Science hasn't got the answer yet, maybe it never will have it, but it seems that motivation or ambition; the will to survive and prosper, is the essence of life.

Meantime we have to be satisfied with the negative definition that life is whatever it is that disappears when a living thing, even a blade of grass, dies. One minute it's crisp and alive, next it is limp and dead; what is it that has gone? Nobody knows. It used to be called 'the soul'.

This question of motivation, will, or ambition is central in the process of evolution by natural selection. It looks us in the face when, with a click, we understand that evolution is essentially a weeding process: one in which all living creatures evolve as their ambition, or will is opposed by external attrition, leaving only the fittest to survive. So, the unknown origin of motivation, will, or ambition is not a trivial question; without it there would be no natural selection. It seems that even Darwin took the origin of ambition in all living things for granted in what he called 'the struggle for existence'.

155

If cooperation did not enhance the performance of one or more of these life-functions it could never have evolved. In other words, the purpose of any cooperative behaviour in any species must lie in helping to improve its performance of one, two or all three of these motives, or life-functions. The ambition to do them is central in this essay. It seems to be almost the definition of life itself. The ambition to survive and prosper is what ceases, vanishes, when a living thing dies. Crucially this applies equally well to a group as it does to an individual.

5. NATURAL SELFISHNESS CAN BE OVERCOME BY GROUP SELECTION

Selfishness fuels the 'struggle for existence' which underpins Darwin's *On the Origin of Species* (1859). To assemble as a cooperating unit, individuals must somehow suppress this powerful imperative. Selfishness is a more essential, more primitive, motivating force than the altruism necessary for cooperation. It's the default mode. Many creatures, such as snakes, butterflies and many fish, survive well without cooperating, but without the self-preservation instinct, without selfishness, every species would quickly become extinct.

Natural selfishness massively opposes the evolution of cooperation. Any creature genetically predisposed to deny itself in order to work with another of the same species thereby gives away a reproductive advantage; meaning that its genes are less likely to be carried into the future. So, any genetic propensity for self-denial in order to cooperate ought to have been promptly weeded out by natural selection. But in co-operators it clearly wasn't. That was the paradox of altruism, and for decades it threatened to upset Darwin's theory of natural selection. However, nature can achieve the difficult trick of getting selfish individuals to cooperate if the group rather than the individual can become the unit which is selected; then it becomes the group that fails or thrives, not the individual. A Russian, Pyotr Kropotkin, was one of the first to have understood this. But Darwin himself had said it in *The Descent of Man* (1871), J. B. S. Haldane developed it further, and then W. D. Hamilton (1964) expressed it in his formula applying to social insects. See 11. The Spark Test below, where levels of selection are discussed.

6. Prioritising between metabolising, self-protection and breeding happens during assembly

The Employee's Tale referred to the observation that work done, by any solitary animal, spider, snake and so on, sub-divides into metabolising, self-protecting and breeding, and that these exact same functions, or versions thereof, comprise the work done by groups. The question then arises: how does a group, using combinations of shouts, grunts, shrieks, moans, eye contact, and other languages, prioritise between these three functions? This prioritisation is simple to a solitary, but how does a group do it? The quick answer is that the prioritisation is done at the assembly stage. In other words, before performance begins.

But it will be pointed out in a review of the interplay between assembly and performance (in PART 2C below) that the reality is not quite so simple, because emotion has the power to sweep rationality aside, even to trigger social breakdown. Here we have the give-and-take dynamic between assembly and performance which was illustrated in video games such as *FIFA* (already mentioned in The Senior Citizen's

Tale). This feedback can be summarised as follows: the work to be done and roles to be played by a group are normally fixed in the process of assembly, or team selection. But dissent and emotion during performance can disrupt a group, especially while it is deciding what plan to adopt. If this happens the re-think that follows can amount to a mini-reassembly. The manager brings on substitutes, or even, at a later stage, buys new players. This illustrates the give-and-take dynamic between assembly and performance.

7. COOPERATE-OR-SPLIT DILEMMA SOLVED BY LANGUAGE-LIKE PROPENSITY

Cooperation in mammals combines genetically inherited propensity with brainpower in order to learn, obey and teach the tribe's culturally established rules of self-restraint. This is a nature-nurture system which works somewhat like language. Thus, inherited propensity explains how a behaviour can evolve by natural selection. There are several well-known variations of this idea, including dual-inheritance theory and genetic sociology. Ernst Meyer referred to it as behaviour being the pacemaker of evolution. In his book *What Evolution Is* (2001), he said:

> A change in behaviour, for instance, adoption of a new food item or increased dispersal, is apt to set up new selection pressures, and these may then lead to evolutionary changes [Mayer 1974]. There are reasons to believe that behavioural shifts have been involved in most evolutionary innovations,

hence the saying 'behaviour is the pacemaker of evolution. Any behaviour that turns out to be of evolutionary significance is likely to be reinforced by selection of genetic determinants for such behaviour (known as the *Baldwin Effect*).

Any creature which evolved a genetic trait for permanent automatic self-restraint, also called altruism, would quickly die out. Clearly any creature thus endowed would be at a competitive disadvantage in the game of reproduction. Altruistic behaviour must be optional, or discretionary, according to the circumstances. This evolution-of-propensity explanation shows how it can be achieved. To repeat the point: It is not altruism that is evolved, it is a propensity; the propensity or willingness to learn, obey, and teach the tribe's culturally established rules for self-restraint.

This cooperate-or-split ability is discretionary or flexible; it harnesses a genetically developed propensity which it compares with the promptings of selfishness. The ability to speak is a similarly harnessed propensity; in this case it is a genetically endowed readiness to learn and speak any language, which is harnessed in social intercourse. Evolved propensity harnessed by circumstance, often called the 'nature/nurture' process, occurs frequently in nature.

Social mammals out hunting nicely illustrate the flexibility of this propensity. The question they are solving continuously and effortlessly is, 'Do I cooperate here or split?' In cooperating microbes and insects this question is solved by genetically fixed characteristics such as inheritance and caste systems, but in social mammals it is optional/discretionary. The individual hunter senses that cooperating fully could mean losing out personally: 'I might get injured, but then splitting here would weaken the group.'

One has only to watch a TV documentary on the lifestyle of African wild-dogs out hunting, nursing and playing to see this instinct-plus-learning process in full swing. Puppies are born with a genetically inherited, language-like predisposition for social discipline. It is a system in which, using a propensity, genetically endowed for this purpose, they quickly learn to accept their parents' rules of behaviour, sometimes adding useful inventions of their own. Then in play and social experiment youngsters try out alternative tactics such as brawling, bullying, boasting, running away, aggression, self-restraint, greed, cheating and sharing fairly. They learn about balancing social ambition against personal safety, and nonconformists get punished or bullied into accepting culturally established tribal rules.

Frans de Waal described this behaviour in 'The Animal Roots of Human Morality', an article on chimpanzees in the *New Scientist*:

Let me recount a fascinating situation that I witnessed years ago at Arnhem Zoo in the Netherlands. One balmy evening when the keeper called the large chimpanzee colony inside, two adolescent females refused to enter the building. The weather was superb, they had the whole island to themselves and were loving it. The zoo's rule was that none of the apes would get fed until they had all moved inside. The obstinate teenagers threw the rest of the group into a grumpy mood. When they finally came in, they were assigned a separate bedroom by the keeper to prevent reprisals.

> This protected them only temporarily, though. The next morning, out on the island, the entire colony vented its frustration about the delayed meal by a mass pursuit ending in a beating for the culprits. That evening, the same two females were the first to come in.
>
> *New Scientist*, 14 October 2006, p. 61

Apart from the use of propensity, uniquely, by mammals, several other assembly mechanisms are usually at play in varying combinations among all cooperating animals including microbes. The African wild dog, as well as using its propensity for rules, also makes use of quorum-sensing and caste systems. Humans do so too, and the use of brainpower to keep track of these social dynamics explains how a mammal tribe creates cultural tramlines, maintains them and passes them on to future generations. (The tramlines of culture are described in PART 3 below).

Genetically inherited social propensity shows why the altruism dilemma which confronted early Darwinism is a non-problem to dolphins, chimpanzees and other cooperating mammals. The 'cooperate-or-split' mode-switch can be made in an intuitive millisecond; individuals will sometimes get it wrong, but genetic propensity plus education ensure that the working team functions adequately. That is how mammal team members can selectively override their selfish ambition in willing harmony so that the job gets done.

Humans are no different in this. We are cooperating mammals. We are not born with a ready-made language such as Chinese or Greek but with a genetic propensity to learn, practice and speak any language.

Similarly, we learn to build up personal mental reference libraries of social response habits which are more-or-less appropriate to our own particular circumstances and individual abilities.

C. L. Apicella and others described these processes in *Nature* magazine (26/1/12) in their article 'Social Networks and Cooperation in Hunter-Gatherers'. Assembly will never be perfect, nor will performance, but genetic propensity explains how society is maintained and how individuals manage to muddle by in it. Pierre Bourdieu's concept of what he called '*habitus*', describes how a human individual becomes socialised, reacting instinctively according to disposition and experience. C. G. A. Bryant offered the following translation from the French of Bourdieu's eloquent, and thoughtful, description of *habitus*:

> The *habitus* – embodied history, internalised as second nature and so forgotten as history – is the active presence of the whole past of which it is the product. As such, it is what gives practices their relative autonomy with respect to external determinations of the immediate present. This autonomy is that of the past, enacted and acting, which, functioning as accumulated capital, produces history on the basis of history and so ensures the permanence in change that makes the individual agent a world within a world. The habitus is a spontaneity without consciousness or will, opposed as much to the mechanical necessity of things without history in mechanistic theories as it is to the reflexive freedom of subjects 'without inertia' in rationalist theories.
>
> C. G. A. Bryant, *Practical Sociology*, Polity Press, 1995

I had to read this passage several times before I could understand what Bourdieu meant, it is after all a translation from French, but he has eloquently expressed in some detail what I mean by the 'social response personal reference library', or 'mental reference library' which informs, and is available to, genetic propensity. Bourdieu's *habitus* and my mental library are both essentially descriptions of the same thing. They are descriptions of cultural socialisation. Bourdieu uses it to explain several social dynamics, and especially the structure / agency dilemma, (see below PART 3). I use it to explain the mode switch that enables assembly in mammals.

Genetically inherited propensity demonstrates how a cooperating mammal, using its mental reference library, can switch effortlessly between altruistically assembled team player and selfish solitary; between cooperate and split. It also demonstrates how the mammal can makes this switch for the good of the group; altruistically. This flexibility brings considerable strength in the struggle to survive. In science fiction a flexibly cooperating opponent such as a realistic human is more formidable than a rigid, pre-programmed one such as an ant-woman.

8. GROUPS ACQUIRE QUASI-MINDS

Although syphonophores and Portuguese men o'war clearly don't have minds of their own, nevertheless they aren't exactly mindless. The argument here is that the process of assembly brings a sort of group mind into existence. This acts as a controlling or orchestrating consensus whose purpose is quite simply that for which the group assembled in the first place. This quasi-mind is most developed in mammals, but it exists in the groups that are formed by all cooperating creatures; none of these groups or units is exactly mindless, they all seek to survive and prosper *not as individuals but as groups.*

I have already quoted Gustave Le Bon on quasi-minds in the Introduction. Further work on this was done by Antonio Gramsci, writing in his prison notebooks (1971):

> Every social group, coming into existence on the original terrain of an essential function in the world of economic production, creates together with its self, organically, one or more strata of intellectuals which give it homogeneity and an awareness of its own function not only in the economic but also in the social and political fields.

Gramsci was of course talking about humans, but the same principles apply to other social mammals.

An individual will switch behavioural modes during the process of becoming a cog-in-the-group. Building on Sigmund Freud and his followers, Wilfred Bion (1996) developed the technique of group psychotherapy which uses this mode-switching. In *Experiences in Groups,* (op.cit., page 102), he described the 'proto-minds' of human groups. When a group acts purposely, he said, it behaves as if it has a corporate mind; a mind which tracks progress and is capable of moods such as anxiety, sympathy and aggression. It responds, learns and remembers how to adopt these different attitudes, and these abilities are independent of any individual group member. The leaders have to respect the corporate mind. Furthermore, the tramlines of culture,

PART 2 below, are essential to the workings of a group's quasi-mind; its culture is its memory.

Apart from Gramsci and Bion there are many descriptions of this group quasi-mind in humans. Notable examples include Bernard Mandeville's *The Fable of the Bees*, J. J. Rousseau's *The Will of the People*, Emile Durkheim's 'collective representations' through which society becomes conscious of itself, Swingewood (2000) and William Sumner (1906); these have all affirmed its existence. Anthony King in *The British Journal of Sociology* (2010) documents the flexibility of the quasi-mind of a nation state and its families in the twentieth and twenty-first centuries. Thomas Keneally illustrates the quasi-minds of human groups in *Schindler's Ark* (1982).

Bullying is interesting here; it is dealt with in PART 3 below. The collective emotion of disgust aroused by bullying (Hitler was a good case) is one of several examples supporting the observation that even though a group cannot have a mind, nevertheless it is not exactly mindless. Other examples include collective fear, hysteria, sadness, hubris, and collective joy, and the common thread is that these *mental* processes are all articulated and converted into action by emotion. The distinction is between personal and group cognition. Here is what Wikipedia said on *group cognition* on 31/8/18:

> Group cognition is a social, largely linguistic phenomenon whereby a group of people produce a sequence of utterances that performs a cognitive act . . . The theory of group cognition is a post-cognitivism philosophy, which considers a larger unit of analysis than an individual mind as a producer of cognitive activities such as creative problem solving.

165

While individual mammals are coalescing into a unit, forming a team, they assess the size of the task, and they assess each other. Who is available? Who is best at the work to be done? They divide their labour, allocating jobs, often called roles, according to reputation, willingness and ability, into the best pattern available. Business structures, or 'business models', in industry are a good example; though endlessly variable, their design criteria are always the same; their parameters and architecture, and their trial-and-error feedback loops are always designed simply for commercial success, nothing more, nothing less.

Occasionally a group can lose its way, arguing within itself as to what its real purpose is supposed to be. This can be refreshed by referring back to the assembly stage; the purpose back then was quite clearly that for which the group was being formed. Business structure and job allocation are also just two functions of assembly. They too are best decided before performance begins.

These requirements for purpose, structure and role allocation illustrate the priority of assembly over performance. Within the machinery of social behaviour, assembly precedes and gives rise to the quasi-mind.

9. THE THREE ASSEMBLY MECHANISMS: CASTE SYSTEMS, QUORUMS, AND BRAINPOWER

Evolutionary biologists have so far recognised three main types of mechanism used by social animals to manage their cooperation: 1. Caste systems epitomised by the social insects; human slavery is a type of caste system. 2. Quorum-sensing with cheater detection, which even occurs in social microbes, as described by Stewart A. West (see under Item 10 below). And 3. Brainpower, which is most developed in the social mammals. The complexity of daily transactions in mammal societies is believed to have driven the evolution of their more powerful brains, which among other things are used to handle the social complexities of self-denial, altruism and discretionary give-and-take.

These three methods, castes, quorums/cheaters and brainpower, are used in varying combinations by different creatures to maintain the three different life-functions; metabolisation, self-protection and breeding, and each combination requires some form of communication, so it's a very complicated three-dimensional picture.

The possible permutations of these three methods crossed with the three life functions are combined differently in different creatures, so the variety in nature is almost endless. Certain microbes, plants, planktons, cicadas and corals self-protect or breed by mass-production. Humboldt Squid usually work together to get food by mobbing. Some birds and fish protect themselves by flocking or shoaling. Then there are the all-purpose cooperators. These include slime moulds, colonial jellyfish, siphonophores, termites, dolphins, humans and naked mole-rats.

Cooperation occurs between animal species, as in cleaner-fish and client, and between animals and plants, as in heather and bees. Even double cooperation can happen as in one heather plus two bees, plus three human beekeepers.

Nature doesn't think ahead, it merely evolves a trait as far as it is immediately useful; snakes, praying mantises, frogs, bears and tigers get along very well as solitaries. And doubtless some species living today have ancestors who cooperated in the distant past but have since lost that ability when it ceased to be an advantage; like blind fish living in the total darkness of underground cave systems. This dizzying, three-dimensional, array of exquisitely tuned and combined ways to cooperate was comprehensively surveyed by, among others, E. O. Wilson in *Sociobiology* (1975) so I will concentrate on mammals and particularly humans.

10. COOPERATE OR SPLIT: SWITCHING MODES OF BEHAVIOUR

An Olympic rowing eight looks like one single creature, smooth and powerful, its eight legs perfectly coordinated. This perfection, even when the crew is exhausted, is what makes it so boring to watch. Each oarsman has voluntarily subordinated his individuality to the crew; three minutes before, he was a proud athlete wearing those trendy sunglasses, trying to impress the girls, but now he loyally and selflessly throws his lot in with his mates. The crew-as-a-unit fits him in as a cog in a greedy machine, a ruthless unit which just wants to win. Without thought, crew members slide or switch their modes of behaviour between self-conscious individual and team player. The slide is effortless and subconscious. Other slide-about examples include wolves and humpback whales out hunting, Hitler's Nazi party, and the Boston Symphony Orchestra. We are all switching and sliding modes all the time; we do it when we go to work. Georg Simmel writing in 1892 described the switching of modes as a process in which human individuals form groups or 'sociated forms' to satisfy their joint interests (A. Swingewood, 2000).

During the pandemic Lock Down imposed during April 2020, the whole of the British Isles was asked to stand at their doors or windows

at 8.00pm every Thursday and demonstrate their thanks for the h efforts of the NHS by clapping. It felt a thoroughly embarrassing even an 'un-British' activity, but my grandson Oliver and I forced other to participate. As soon as we began, a strange thing happ Our cringing embarrassment evaporated in a sort of catharsis as pleasure in this group activity took over. I later realised that the v experience was an excellent demonstration of what I have calle 'cooperate-or-split-switch.'

This mode switching even occurs in cooperating microbes; clearly described by Stewart A. West in the podcast of his 19/1/0 to the Royal Society. West explained how in *Pseudomonas aerugina* release by individuals of small signalling molecules can tell other iduals that a quorum for cooperation may exist. A mode-switch solitary to co-operator can then be triggered in these tiny individu

This is an especially important point in assembly and perfori thinking. It shows that the same essential functions which cooperation can be observed in microbes, in the social insec mammals, and in fact in all animal co-operators, not just in hu This must be the case; because if all animals are endowed with r selfishness, it has to be overcome before cooperation is possible.

Like birds in flight staying airborne, cooperation must be ke meaning that in social mammals the default condition is solit; humans, cooperation is a daily achievement. I wake up every m as a selfish solitary, then I may or may not subordinate myse working group: 'Will I cooperate, or will I split?' When fully asse or incorporated I will become an indiscriminate cog in a group has a sort of mind, a quasi-mind, of its own.

Assembly can be disrupted. That's because it is a distinct pl

which must be achieved before cooperation can proceed. Humans do disruption in medicine when simple hygiene prevents sundry species of quorum-sensing social microbes from incorporating into breeding communities. In humans, police-work during public demonstrations nicely illustrates the disruption of assembly; if this fails riots can quickly spread.

In the case of ants and termites, caste systems are used to assemble the whole colony; assembly is fixed by the queen, individuals do not have the option to cooperate or split and that includes the queen. She is trapped, imprisoned even. In mammals, assembly, with rare exceptions such as the naked mole-rat (described above in The Mother's Tale) is usually a matter of individual choice and is mainly achieved by brainpower. But any animal species which cooperates must always, somehow, have evolved techniques for overcoming natural selfishness.

Mode-switching in humans can explain bullying, gang warfare, bureaucracy, law making, morality, and corporate greed. These are discussed below in PART 3.

In cooperating microbes and social insects, mode-switching is genetically ordained, colonially fixed, slavishly automatic. The individual slime-mould cell, Portuguese man o' war cell, or wasp, doesn't think to itself, 'Hmm ... brother or cousin? I'll help here if it's my brother but if it's only my cousin I won't risk it.' (See Hamilton's rb > c rule and game theory below). But in mammals it is conscious and optional. Conscious here means being self-aware and using brainpower to weigh up the costs of failure against the benefits of success. The cooperating mammal – dolphin, vampire bat, human, or hyena – must notice the multitude of daily social transactions flickering

through its group, and it must understand and learn from them; in this process, brainpower enables it to understand a loose version of W. D. Hamilton's rb > c family relationship calculation.

The members of a rowing eight switch modes effortlessly, without conscious thought. Years ago, in their primary school playgrounds, they learnt the manoeuvres of gang warfare. Cooperate or switch decision-making may be a split-second instinct in the oarsman, wolf and elephant, but these arguments demonstrate that biologically it is a highly evolved and complex ability.

As already described in argument 7 above, this ability to switch modes has been evolved in cooperating mammals in a manner similar to the evolution of language.

11. THE SPARK TEST: ONLY TWO LEVELS OF SELECTION

In nature nothing stands still, situations evolve. Weather systems evolve and so do land masses. Evolution by natural selection is one special type of evolution. It is essentially a weeding process, one in which many aspirants face attritional forces with the result that only the 'fittest' survive and reproduce. This requires, on the one hand a life-form motivated by the ambition to metabolise, self-protect and breed, and on the other a destructive attritional force: the weeding agent. This process also requires that these forces, or elements actually do confront each other. This live-or-die confrontation is the essence of the weeding process. It is like the spark in a petrol engine: no confrontation – no weeding.

OK, so now we can ask: at what level of life does natural selection take place; where does it spark? Is it the gene, the individual, the tribal group or the whole species? Current scholarship, notably by S. Pinker, R. Dawkins, S. Okasha, E. Wilson and others seems to favour multi-level selection in which natural selection operates at several levels at the same time. As many as nine levels of selection have been proposed, these are: Gene, Chromosome, Seed, Tissue, Organ, Individual, Group, Species, Ecosystem; but if the focal point of the whole business is where ambition meets attrition, the process cannot select or spark if either is absent. The question as to which of these nine levels the selection process operates at puts a spotlight on the ambition element of the spark. Where does the ambition lie? Natural ambition is embodied in every living life-form, even if dormant in a seed. It is always absent in a life-form that has died. Matter at the first five of these levels of organisation: gene, chromosome, seed, tissue and organ is inert. Inert here means not having whatever it is, ambition I call it, that vanishes when the life-form in question dies. For example, when a gene, seed, or organ dies or decays, ambition cannot be said to disappear, because none existed in the first place. Admittedly metabolism does proceed in organs preserved for transplant but only mechanically/automatically, as in a hydraulic ram pump. In other words, such tissues have no ambition, they are inert. Organisms that do not 'want' to metabolise, self-protect and breed are in this sense inert; they have no natural ambition, and cannot be units of selection. Sorry to belabour the point but if there is no ambition there can be no spark.

If, however, it can be accepted that not only individuals but also cooperating groups or social units, termite mounds and chimpanzee tribes possess ambitious quasi-minds then they pass the spark test and qualify as units of selection.

A way of arguing this point is to ask at each level: Where is the essence of life? Where is the ambition which disappears at death? The answers rule out all levels other than individual and group.

An esoteric case might be made that whole species and ecosystems could qualify as units of selection, but these, not even possessing quasi-minds, cannot be said to have natural ambition. This means that only individuals and groups can spark in the 'combustion-chambers' of evolution by natural selection. It is only in these two arenas that the process of evolution by natural selection, or ambition versus attrition, can proceed. And, by the way, selection can proceed simultaneously at both individual and group level.

This argues against the idea that genes, as in Richard Dawkins's 'selfish gene', can be units of selection; they have no ambition. The claim that natural selection can somehow be played out at gene level is analogous to saying that the evolution of language is all about an imaginary competition between the letters of an alphabet. Bur that's not how it works; a language develops by the continual invention of the most useful new sounds, gestures, words, phrases and slang, and by the attritional weeding out of those which are less useful, less fit for the purpose of communication. And communication is the sole purpose of language. This weeding spark happens when words, new and old, are tested for their comprehension value. The competition is between words; that's where the weeding takes place, it's not between the letters of the alphabet. Similarly, in animals the weeding, the natural selection, takes place at the level of the individual or the group but not the genes; they don't have ambition.

Until it can be explained how cooperation evolved from the default or solitary condition we cannot claim to understand 'how society works': which is the subject of this book. So, the validity of group selection is central here; it explains how altruistic cooperation can evolve out of a solitary species despite the massive obstacle of natural selfishness.

12. HAMILTON'S RULE IS NOT THE ANSWER, NEITHER IS GAME THEORY NOR SOCIAL NETWORK ANALYSIS (SNA)

From its beginning, the doctrine of natural selection was haunted by the paradox that altruism ought to be weeded out; it ought to be impossible. This was finally solved by William Hamilton's (1964) explanation of 'inclusive fitness', which he demonstrated in social insects: wasps, termites and so on. What he proposed amounts to an imaginary weighing scales in which individuals will cooperate when benefit outweighs cost. His brilliant formula says that cooperative genes should increase in frequency when rb-c is greater than zero where:

r (relatedness) = the genetic relatedness of the recipient to the actor, often defined as the probability that a gene picked randomly from each at the same locus is identical by descent:

b (benefit) = the additional reproductive benefit gained by the recipient of the altruistic act:

c (cost) = the reproductive cost to the individual of performing the act.

The letter r here is a diluent: a brother halves the calculation and a first cousin quarters it. Though developed originally for the social insects, the formula applies metaphorically to all co-operators, including humans. It is called 'inclusive fitness' because the survival of

174

a co-operator species depends as much on the fitness of its groups as it does on that of its individuals, demonstrating how altruism can be genetically stable.

However, the evolution of assembly from the default, solitary, condition is not addressed by Hamilton's rule. Attempts to do so would collapse in circular argument because the rule must assume, as a given, the prior achievement of assembly. Hamilton's rule does indeed explain the genetic stability of altruism in society despite natural selfishness, but not how social assembly occurs in the first place.

Another way to argue this point is to look forward instead of back; life will go on and creatures will evolve into the future. One of today's solitaries, let's say a species of snake or a solitary slug or snail, could well evolve the ability to cooperate; indeed, that's quite likely. But if it were to do so, this ability could never have been kick-started by Hamilton's rule. Hamilton's rule is a formula indicating the likelihood of continuing cooperation, not its origin.

The origin must lie somewhere in the creature's breeding arrangements. Solitaries are not born recognising their brothers and sisters; first they must somehow evolve the habit of staying together as adults, for mutual benefit. And for this they have to overcome their natural selfishness; they must evolve a combination of caste systems, quorum sensing, cheater detection and genetically inherited propensities.

Game theory has a similar problem: it cannot, as is sometimes suggested, explain the evolutionary origin of cooperation, it too must assume the prior existence of society. Origination claims such as these again amount to circular argument.

Game theory goes back to the 1700s. In the 1950s it was developed into a spectacularly successful tool in sociology. The best known of these is *The Prisoner's Dilemma*. Like Hamilton's rule these models show how altruism can be genetically stable in a social population. There is a variety of highly ingenious social gaming models, many incorporating the use of real money, which explain the emergence of different social behaviours. But when these models claim to describe the origins of society, they fall short because they all must assume the prior achievement of assembly. As Raimo Tuomela pointed out in his book *The Philosophy of Society* (Oxford, 2007, p. 7), the prisoner's dilemma 'simply does not exist – at least on the group-member level – if the group members really act fully as a group'. To put this the other way round; if there is no assembly there can be no dilemma. Solitaries don't play games.

To summarise these arguments: natural selfishness massively opposes the evolution of altruism, but cooperation is widespread in nature, so clearly this barrier has been overcome many times. However, neither Hamilton's rule nor game theory can, as is sometimes claimed, explain the evolutionary origin of cooperation. This is because they both must assume the prior existence of society. Whenever such claims are made, they amount to circular arguments. Both of these doctrines are brilliant explanations of how cooperation can flourish in nature despite natural selfishness. But neither of them can explain how it arose in the first place. They can't explain how, more or less from its very beginning, life evolved to exploit the pre-existing niche of cooperation. To explain this, it is necessary to research the evolution of breeding methods, caste systems, quorum sensing, cheater detection, and genetically inherited propensities. I have alluded to these already and it is probably enough here to note the extensive research on these matters by Stuart West, Laurent Keller, Tim Cutton-Brock, Alan Grafen, Jacobus Boomsma, Francis Ratnieks, David Queller and others.

13. Hubris, philosophy and economics deceive us into taking assembly for granted

The human is highly social, and with our sociality comes a self-reinforcing tendency to take pride in, and glorify, the quasi-mind of our tribe. This feeds back into and strengthens the bonds and navigation processes that enable us to succeed as a species. But as we saw in The Mother's Tale, success can breed complacency, and when corporate success introduces too much self-satisfied pride or hubris, that's when we start to lose sight of ourselves and begin to take our ability to assemble working teams for granted.

For example, this can happen when we are over-impressed by dubious but comfortable ideas about the unique status of mankind, it then becomes easy to assume that *because Homo sapiens is supreme, it is the supreme co-operator.* Actually, top of the league table of co-operators come the siphonophores, the slime moulds and other 'colonial creatures', then below them and before *Homo sapiens* come the ants and the naked mole-rats. Their cooperation is tighter, more 'evolved' than ours.

Hubris deflects sociologists from asking about why *Homo sapiens* can assemble, or how we do it; these seem pointless questions. We are a brilliantly social animal, the argument goes, therefore society exists; that much is obvious, what's the point in asking why or how we do it? And anyway, it has all been adequately explained by philosophers, economists, and evolutionary biologists, so sociologists need not bother too much about Darwin. I suggest that both philosophy and economics need to be questioned more closely on this:

....

- Philosophy is underpinned in our folk-law by the tacit acceptance that wise men, and scholars, using their personal brainpower, can, by introspection, work out what our individual, personal, lives are all about, and how best to live them. They deal with things like ethics, meaning, being-and-existence and consciousness. But their findings seldom probe the functioning of teams; they do not normally consider the functioning of the tribe's quasi-mind. Being about *individual* mentality only, classical philosophy ignores the workings of *group* mentality. As I have already said in the Introduction: though groups clearly don't have minds as such, they are not exactly mindless. But philosophy prefers to take the machinery of group minds for granted.

- Economics is similarly hampered. As we saw in The Student's Tale, (PART 1 above) classical economics is based on the tacit assumption that society is made up of individuals, *homo economicae*, who pursue their individual benefits. Classical economics ignores the fact that groups, which also pursue their own selfish benefits, can produce quite different, but also greedy or cruel, outcomes. Classical economics further assumes that, using statistics, realistic models of society can be constructed on this 'multitude of self-seeking individuals' assumption. Unfortunately, social groups are much less amenable to statistical manipulation. For this reason, classical

178

economics finds it more convenient to take the human's ability to assemble its 'unique sociality', for granted.

....

It's not until we remember Darwin's chapter on 'the struggle for existence' in his *On the Origin of Species*, and Kropotkin's question about the ubiquity of altruism, that it seems sensible, before wondering how society works, to question its very existence. If the default position of all animals is natural selfishness, which massively opposes altruism, how can it be that teams are even able to assemble in the first place? It's not good enough to take the ability to assemble into working teams for granted. We need to understand how it's done before tackling the question of how these teams go about their tasks. And it so happens that when we work that one out, surprise, surprise, it becomes clear that the mechanisms of assembly are quite different from those of performance. This distinction only becomes obvious when we first examine how assembly can be possible. What I am saying in this book is that assembly and performance thinking, which is about the group not the individual, seriously undermines both classical philosophy and classical economics.

This perception is not normally available to us unless we first abandon the hubristic attitude, tacitly assumed by philosophy, that the human is a superior animal, now existing in a completely separate category of its own. This attitude opens the following circular trap:

....

- The human is superior, unique in category among all other animals. Only it can study itself philosophically.

- Philosophy takes our supremely social nature as given.

- So, there is little point in wondering how it is that human individuals are able to assemble in cooperation, or indeed, when they do, how they do it.

- This ability is a given, taken for granted; it is the very essence of our human uniqueness.

....

I'm saying here that for the past two or three centuries at least, whenever we have studied the workings of society, we have been bamboozled, first by philosophy and then by economics, into ignoring the crucial difference between the way in which individuals assemble into working groups and the way in which these groups perform their tasks.

August Comte and Emile Durkheim proposed a scientifically objective analysis of society, but their objectivity tended to ignore the more miserable effects of the Industrial Revolution. It was quickly swept aside as unkind and heartless by the more humanistic scholarship of Max Weber, Georg Simmel and Karl Marx. Western sociology today is a grand mixture of both approaches, but it is still more concerned with normative remedies than the biological principles of our animal nature.

Objective sociology seems to have been swamped by benevolent, or 'normative', humanism. Sociology today spends its time trying to put wrongs to right before understanding how society actually works. At our gossip centres: local pub, dining table, village hall and school gate, we are still content with beliefs in which the human is at the centre of the cosmos. That's hubris. Maybe we need to bring ourselves down to earth with a dose of realism spiced with a touch of humility. We could start by teaching our children about assembly. Assembly is after all a remarkable achievement and, as I try to argue in PART 3 below, it is very much more important for our welfare than sex education.

14. We need humility, not hubris

I have tried to argue that we must side-step the hubris built into classical philosophy and economics before we can understand how the difficult trick of assembly despite natural selfishness is achieved. The way is then clear for us to examine the totally different question of how groups perform. That comes next.

PART 2

SOCIAL THEORY PERFORMANCE

PERFORMANCE

If these arguments about assembly can be accepted, then let us examine the mechanisms of performance. As I have already said they are quite different. The first thing to say is that without accommodating emotion, no theory of social performance can be complete. Disappointment, fear, panic, pride and triumph can quickly spread among people. When this happens, emotion can disrupt group performance; even wreck it completely; forcing the reassembly or even the permanent destruction of a cooperating unit. The social damage caused by emotion will be discussed PART 2 Interplay Triggered by Emotion.

The Frog and Heron

When an individual acting alone does something purposeful, the action proceeds by trial and error. In fact, it is more accurate to say that it proceeds in three phases: plan, act and review. Planning here is essential to set up the next action, otherwise the individual is doomed to repeat the error in perpetuity. In other words, purposeful individuals, be they solitaries or social creatures, but acting alone, must always perform this feedback control loop, which they repeat as necessary to get any job done. This rule of three can be used to describe individual performance.

star = plan, whirl = act, book = review

Even plants and microbes follow this rule of performance. Microbes inhabit their surroundings by fast breeding. One individual split's itself in two, each of which then split again, making four. Very quickly this multiplication could produce an enormous population. They have no brains so individuals cannot prioritise or economise, but life to them is cheap and as they swarm about, doing their thing, natural selection, with mutation, proceeds at individual level, played out over many fast-breeding generations.

It's a simple and effective performance strategy; instead of planning how to boil one egg you boil millions hoping that at least one will be OK. That is how with the help of natural selection certain bacteria have been able to out-perform antibiotics.

Next comes navigation with prioritisation. More evolved solitary animals, having developed learning as a brain function, can be said to 'navigate' their surroundings. Each one learns and remembers as it goes, and memory enables it to prioritise its performance between metabolising, self-protection and breeding.

A frog, for example, being a solitary creature, messes about continually doing its life functions: eating, breathing, and eliminating waste, looking out for danger and searching for mates. Presented with opportunities and threats in any of these functions it decides with the help of memory which of the three is most compelling 'right now'. Then it performs or acts purposefully iterating a cybernetic feedback control loop. The frog cycles rapidly and continuously through its act > check result > readjust, > act again > and repeat, continuing as necessary. This comprises the set of mechanisms at work in a solitary animal's performance. I call it the rule of three.

Reverse trumping, where for example in readjusting the frog ignores what it learnt when 'result-checking', could be fatal (reverse trumping is described further in PART 2 Interplay Triggered by Emotion below). When a heron looms overhead, the frog gives self-protection priority over its eating. It leaps to escape the fearsome beak, thinking 'Phew, that was close!' It learns and remembers the importance of keeping a constant look-out and of knowing where the best hiding places are. Thus, the frog's brain prioritises the conflicting imperatives to metabolise, self-protect and breed. And as it performs what it considers the most urgent of these three imperatives it iterates the triangular cybernetic navigation control loop: The Rule of Three.

In humans this brainwork is part of what we introspectively think of as consciousness; we know we are doing it. Who knows whether frogs introspect? My guess is that they must at least have a sense of self, because if they could not perform the prioritisation function, which we can see them doing, they would quickly go extinct. I belong to the school which thinks that, in humans, consciousness is merely the feeling we have that we are aware that we are aware that we are aware: a philosophical feeling. Frogs do not eat their own fingers.

The Rule of Three Summarised as It Applies to Individual Performance

Individual animals, both primitive and evolved, when acting alone, perform as follows: They plan what to do next, execute the plan, and then review the new situation before revising the plan. A frog, a solitary, acting by its 'trial and error' process iterates to a feedback control loop consisting of three phases: plan> act > review > and plan again.

Even individual microbes can do rudimentary reviewing or learning. This process is elegantly described by Denis Bray in his book *Wetware* (2009). In animals with brains, learning involves remembering the best way of doing things, for use next time. Performance requires balancing best methods against expectations in the business of meta-bolising, self-protecting and breeding. Each phase specifies, or trumps, the next, like the game 'scissors, paper and stone', where scissors cut paper, paper wraps stone and stone blunts scissors.

The rather grand claim here is that this rule describes the perform-ance of all living things, including plants and microbes, and that optimum performance is that which best conforms to this rule. The logic of the 'Rule of Three' demonstrates that though more than three phases are clumsily possible, logically the optimum is always three phases: not more and not less. The rule simply requires 1. that the three mutually trumping parameters are selected, and 2. that their order of trumping is fixed. Though this rule applies to all animal performance, it is developed here as a tool for analysing group rather than individual performance.

The Rule of Three Applies Mainly to Groups when Acting as One Creature

The question here is primarily about groups: not individuals. How do groups perform? How do they get their jobs done? Who is running the show? How actually does society work? The answer offered here is that the same triangular feedback control loop is at work in the group, as in the individual. Furthermore, it is argued that this applies without exception to all social creatures on earth. Leadership is a simple but sweeping device. The individual social mammal notices: 'Hey, look! An opportunity! Come on everybody! Let's go,' triggering performance, or loop iteration, at group level.

As Stuart West showed, (see page 169 above) even social microbes do quorum sensing. Once individuals are alerted and a group is assembled, the same mechanisms which operate individual performance can be seen to swing into action. The continual iteration of the loop in pursuit of its purpose is orchestrated by the group's quasi-mind.

This communal mind came into being during assembly, (see above; 'Groups acquire quasi-minds,' page 163). If, for example, the agreed purpose is to improve food supply by building a bridge; this is what has triggered the assembly of the group in the first place. This agreed purpose then presides over the performance of the group when acting as a unit. Cooperating mammals intra-communicate communal moods and emotions such as triumph, pride, anger, anxiety, fear, panic, hysteria and torpor. These flickering quasi-mind 'messages' motivate the group.

Except in major events and disturbances, such as earthquakes, epidemics, and forest fires, these corporate moods do not spread beyond group boundaries. Leadership is often an important feature of group behaviour, but it is always ultimately subservient to the group quasi-mind. According to the Rule of Three it is trumped by popular opinion, gossip and so on. All three phases of the loop are orchestrated by the group quasi-mind. There are certain life forms where ultra-tight cooperation makes the group look just like one individual. E. O. Wilson calls these units Superorganisms. Examples from his *Sociobiology* include the Portuguese man o' war, siphonophores and the slime moulds. In these creatures the will to survive and prosper has become corporate; it was what triggered the evolution of these extraordinary colonial life-forms in the first place.

E. O. Wilson describes the behaviour of the slime mould Dictyostelium discoideum.

The biology of Dictyostelium and related slime moulds has been perceptively reviewed by Bonner (1967, 1970) one of the chief contributors to its study.

The Dictyostelium cycle can be conveniently marked as beginning with the setting of spores into the soil, leaf litter or rotting wood. The emerging cells are single-celled and behave like 'true' amebas; they creep through liquid films, engulfing bacteria and dividing at frequent intervals. The cells are completely independent of one another so long as a rich supply of food is available. When the food grows scarce, however, a dramatic change occurs. Certain amebas become attraction centers, and the remainder of the population streams toward them. Soon the random array is transfigured into rosettes of amebas, with a rising center and radiating arms composed of the amebas still migrating inward. As the aggregation congeals further it assumes a sausage shape averaging ½ to 2 millimeters in length. This new entity, called a pseudoplasmodium or grex, now performs like a multicellular organism. It has distinct front and hind ends and moves slowly in the direction of heat and light. Up to one or two weeks later the pseudoplasmodium transforms into a fruiting body, with some of the former amebas contributing to base and stalk and others to the spore-bearing spheres at the tip. Each species of cellular slime mould has a distinctive version of this final, most complex life stage.

E. O. Wilson, *Sociobiology*, Harvard, 2008, p. 388

Another example of superorganism behaviour, this time by honeybees, was written up in *Nature Physics*, doi.org/ct3g. This work was then described in the *New Scientist*, page 19, issue 319729, September 2018. A swarm of honeybees hanging from a branch can change its shape in bad weather. Now we know more about how the bees work as a single superorganism to do this. There is no step-break in the evolution of all animal species ranging from solitary to superorganism from microbe to human. Furthermore, they all, without exception perform the same three life functions: acquiring energy, self-protection and breeding. This supports my claim that the same system of plan > execute > review operates in the performance of all social units just as it does in all solitaries. It is a three-phase, mutually trumping, cybernetic feedback, navigation control loop. No other logic is available for the business of performance by living things.

If at first these explanations seem somewhat abstract it may be worth noting in their defence that they are no less abstract than the now classical principles of Keynsian economics. Getting used to novelty sometimes takes a little time.

Groups Do Things the Same Way as Solitaries

Time for a quick summary. The animal kingdom ranges from the amoebae to mammals, and the ability to cooperate has been evolved independently by many different species throughout this range. Types of cooperation vary according to the purpose for which each was evolved. Many animals get along very well without cooperation; nature's default condition is solitary. The purposes of cooperation can be either metabolism, self-protection or breeding, or any combination of these. There is thus a bewildering array of cooperation in the animal kingdom. This array can then be further extended into inter-species cooperation. The social animals have been much researched in recent years by evolutionary biologists, including E. O. Wilson whose wonderfully comprehensive book *Sociobiology – the New Synthesis* (1975) was one of the first in the field.

The claim here is that a unifying order can be imposed on this kaleidoscopic picture of animal cooperation, and that this can be done in two steps. The first is to recognise that, as described above in PART 2a, selfish individuals have collected together for a purpose: they have had to assemble. Obvious? Yes. But simple? No. The second step is to recognise that each, and every one of these animal assemblies performs its purpose according to the same universal logic, loosely known as trial and error. I call it 'The Rule of Three'. This is very simply the perpetual cycle of review > plan > execute > repeat. It is described in painstaking detail below (see The Rule of Three: A ten-part technical review, page 195).

Given that all animals without exception are driven by the will or ambition to survive and prosper, and thus to process energy, self-protect and reproduce, then the essential features of their performances must necessarily be similar throughout the whole spectrum of animal life. So, it seems legitimate to start the enquiry with a human acting alone, as in boiling an egg. Here the moves are easy to see. One can then infer that the same trial-and-error sequence of moves must also apply when human groups perform work, as in getting a fallen tree out of a river for example. That in turn may show us how society works. If this simple bit of reasoning can be falsified, then my assembly and performance thinking collapses.

SUMMARIES: one brief and one more technical

The Rule of Three is central in assembly and performance thinking. So that it can be criticised and examined for flaws, here is a short summary, followed by a more technical, 10-part review.

....

1. Unity is essential to the success of a social unit.

2. In humans, every social unit – family, racing eight, choir, working party, military platoon and business corporation – has its own quasi-mind orchestrating its Rule of Three.

3a. 'Plan' trumps or triggers 'act'; autocrats are scared of gossip because individual members' opinions can unite them to oppose leadership policy.

3b. 'Act' triggers a new review, because the results of the latest action modify conditions and alter the tramlines of group cultural memory.

3c. 'Review' in the form of cultural memory, trumps or constrains 'plan': without one specific language, or one standardised road-traffic system, there would be chaos; cultural tramlines are essential to society.

....

The Rule of Three: a ten-part technical review

The Rule of Three claims to be a logic of performance, displaying the sequence of steps taken by social animals when they work together. The explanations and arguments below are offered as a target for critics to shoot at. If they survive this ordeal, they may help to show how assembly and performance thinking could clarify the enigma of human society, with its corporate greed and genocide alongside benevolence. The Rule of Three has already been referred to in several different contexts above. There now follows a complete, and inevitably repetitive, description grouped into ten arguments.

1. THE RULE IS MORE RELEVANT TO GROUPS THAN TO INDIVIDUALS

This Rule of Three applies primarily to the performance of groups. It does also apply to individuals but is less relevant to them since individuals have powerful, nimble minds of their own. A mammal acting alone can cut corners and react intuitively; it can 'float like a butterfly and sting like a bee' (Muhammad Ali, 1964) but a mammal group cannot do that. Groups only have quasi-minds. Such thought processes as they may have, are corporate, primitive and rudimentary. The difference is similar to the difference between a terrorist network and a standing army: terrorists can cut corners, they hit and vanish; armies follow traditional rules of warfare, they strategise and manoeuvre ponderously.

2. DESCRIPTION OF THE RULE INCLUDING SELF-MOTIVATION

The rule of three consists of the following three mutually trumping performance parameters: review > plan > execute > repeat. It is the name given to one particular type of control loop. It is superficially like the game 'scissors, paper, and stone'. The claim here is that this rule describes the performances of all animal cooperating groups. Fully described, it is a mutually trumping, internally motivated, cybernetic, triangular, feedback control loop, in which iteration proceeds without external input. It is a system whose self-motivation, orchestrated by its quasi-mind, is derived, through assembly, out of the ambition which life somehow endows on inert matter; (see: The evolutionary origin of cooperation above).

This self-motivation is an important characteristic in the animal cooperating groups we see daily from ants and crows to humans. They are all self-motivated. Not one of the many types of human group – families, villages, business companies, charities, sports clubs and multinationals – is motivated by external inputs. They react to external events of course but they are self-motivated to do so. In this they differ categorically from the many types of cybernetic, negative-feedback control loops used for example in rocket science and driverless cars. The self-motivation in animal cooperating groups comes from their quasi-minds: minds which came into being during assembly. Rockets are not alive, nor are cars. To repeat: the three mutually trumping parameters or functions are always subservient to the will or ambition of the group quasi-mind. This ambition was what triggered the assembly of the group in the first place. Ambition specifies the group's overall purpose, which in turn specifies its three mutually trumping parameters or functions.

3. THE RULE OF THREE IS MERELY AN OPTIMUM

The Rule of Three is merely an optimum. It is an ideal pattern, or blueprint. The specific parameters in use for any purpose can be varied according to circumstances. In fact, the rule is quite often broken; this happens, for example, when the irrational force of emotion sweeps through a group; knocking rationality aside (as already described in PART 1 The Mother's Tale and also The Senior Citizen's Tale). Real life abounds with exceptions to rules; two parameters are indeed possible and so are four or more. For example, four parameters can occur in a fluid situation such as Kurt Lewin's spiral, (described below). The Rule of Three is an a priori mathematical ideal; cooperating groups which try to operate less or more than three parameters in their constitutions invite confusion and lose competitive fitness thereby.

4. THE RULE IS A PRIORI; WITH NO LESS AND NO MORE THAN THEE IDEAL FUNCTIONS

Logically there cannot be less than three functions in an ideal feedback control loop; If there are only two, performance cannot progress, it is trapped permanently in a groove, hunting back and forth between two phases. A third phase is necessary to avoid this trap. The game cannot be played with only scissors and paper. Furthermore, there cannot be more than three functions in the system. More than three functions in a social system would introduce the quandary of alternative pathways in the iteration of the loop. If four mutually trumping parameters were built into a national constitution – let's say government > law > army > media >, then there would be no intrinsic way – no way without external input – to prevent media from trumping law as well as government, because media is not trumped by law. Thus, external input is necessary so as to avoid ambiguity and ensure mutual trumping; and then the system is no longer internally motivated However as already noted, the motivation, or ambition, in a rule of three is imposed, internally, by its quasi-mind which came into being at the assembly stage. So ideally there should be only three functions in an internally motivated mutually trumping cybernetic feedback control loop. Never fewer but never more. Any fewer hunts perpetually between the loop's two functions and cannot progress, and any more introduces ambiguity which must be resolved by external intervention. This 'never fewer and never more' statement is mathematically an a priori axiom.

These three categories are a priori in the same sense that Plato's famous ideal forms exist a priori in an ideal, eternal, world of logical, or geometrical principles. The three a priori functions can be given names: A, B and C for example. Here I choose to name them plan, act and review. Media, government and law being mutually trumping fit nicely into these three a priori categories. Given an imaginary tribe orchestrated by the 'survive and prosper' ambition of its quasi-mind, that tribe will perform actions in order to acquire food, protect itself, and rear its young, and these actions will conform to the rule of three. The tribe will plan, execute and review continuously until it ceases to exist. The same is true of any business company. The specific parameters of its control loop will be quite different from those of a tribe, they will suit the type of business it is in, but the same generic functions, plan, execute and review, will prevail. These are descriptions of ideals not rigid rules, but the tribe that best conforms to them over the long term will outcompete its rivals in the ruthless game of survival and prosperity. The game of natural selection.

5. THE SPECIFIC PARAMETERS OF THE RULE ARE HIGHLY VARIABLE

The system proposed here: the performance system of any animal cooperating group, even cooperating microbes, is a triangular, mutually trumping, feedback control loop in which iteration proceeds by self-motivation. All cooperating systems in the living world have variations of these characteristics. They amount to a generic blueprint on which variations are played. Take butterflies, for example. 1. They all fly the same way. 2. They all go through life stages: egg, grub, pupa and adult. 3. They are all insects with six legs. These characteristics are the generic master-pattern or blueprint for butterflies. Within this blueprint butterflies have evolved a wide variety of different life forms. It is much the same with the performance systems in cooperating animals: within the overall master-pattern of plan > execute > review > an almost limitless range of specific parameters is possible. This butterfly example demonstrates the distinction between on the one hand the set of three ideal or generic parameters which apply to all human groups, large or small, Gemeinschaft or Gesellschaft, and on the other the vast number of sets of specifically tailormade parameters used by the vast variety of real-life groups which make up society. Examples of tailor-made parameters of human cooperation include: For business corporations: strategy > act > cash flow > repeat; For a rowing eight: harmony > training > performance-measurement > repeat; For a village cider-making gang: agree method > make the cider > check quality > adjust method for next season > repeat; For a criminal gang: plan crime > commit crime > review success > plan next crime > repeat. For each of the above types of group just one set of very many possible tailor-made parameters is imagined. The point is that within the generic master-pattern each real-life group will operate its own tailor-made triangular, mutually trumping, feedback control loop.

6. ONLY TWO INSTRUCTIONS ARE NECESSARY TO SET UP THE RULE

Only two instructions are needed to set up a rule of three. The first is that the three most potent functions must be selected. And the second is that the order of trumping must be fixed and adhered to thus: A > B > C > A >. But not A > C > B > A >

7. THE SPECIFIC PARAMETERS CAN SPIRAL PROGRESSIVELY: FROM KURT LEWIN

The parameters of a feedback control loop can, and sometimes do, spiral progressively. For example, the three effective parameters may for centuries have been baron > king > church > baron > repeat. But then a rebellion or major defeat in battle can alter, or migrate these, progressively spiralling them into say media > government > law > media. So, though

200

the specific parameters may change in character, and though mini-groups may form and disappear, the permanent logic – the 'plan > execute > review' principle – will always apply. Thus, though the specific parameters may change, the generic blueprint always remains the constant basis of social performance. The following passage is taken from 'Action Research and Minority Problems' by Kurt Lewin, published in the *Journal of Social Sciences*, 1946, 2(4), pp. 34–46.

This reconnaissance or them-finding [after a bombing raid on Nazi German targets] has four functions. First it should evaluate the action. It shows whether what has been achieved is above or below expectation. Secondly it gives the planners a chance to learn, that is to gather new general insight, for instance, regarding the strengths and weakness of certain weapons or techniques of action. Thirdly this fact-finding [I use the word 'review'] should serve as a basis for correctly planning the next step. Finally, it serves as a basis for modifying the overall plan.

The next step again is composed of a circle of planning, executing and reconnaissance or fact-finding [review] for the purpose of evaluating the results of the second step, for preparing the rational basis for planning the third step, and for perhaps modifying the overall plan.

Rational social management, therefore, proceeds in a spiral of steps each of which is composed of a circle of planning, action and fact-finding [review] about the result of that action.

Kurt Lewin's Spiral is essentially the same as the Rule of Three promoted here. They are both trial-and-error systems and both exactly identify the same three functions: review or fact-find, plan, execute, review, repeat. The main differences are in what we use them for.

....

1. Lewin's Spiral was a proposal for running workshops to resolve discrimination against Jews, Hispanic, black and mixed-race people in America, whereas the Rule of Three is the centrepiece of assembly and performance thinking which aims to explain how society works.

2. Assembly and performance thinking relies on the concept of a group quasi-mind presiding over the Rule of Three and ensuring that it pursues the purpose for which the group was assembled in the first place. So, this thinking recognises all animal groups as self-motivated, resisting external interference, whereas Lewin's spiral proposes an externally imposed policy.

3. Lewin did not recognise his spiral as being in use all day, every day, by all animal cooperating groups from microbes, via the social insects to mammals, but assembly and performance thinking does just that, using the concept of the Rule of Three for this purpose.

4. Assembly and performance thinking applies this concept, essentially trial-and-error, to explain that human society works

as a rough-and-tumble of separate cooperating units in more or less harmonious hierarchy. In his 1946 paper Lewin did not venture this far. He died in 1947, aged 57.

....

8. TALCOTT PARSONS PROPOSED A REMARKABLY SIMILAR RULE

Talcott Parsons has already been introduced; see The Student's Tale above, where his AGIL system of social action deals with the same social mechanisms as are described here as the Rule of Three. It may be instructive to compare the two. The passages below, which describe the four elements of Parsons's AGIL scheme, are taken from *Talcott Parsons and American Sociology* by Guy Rocher, pages 45 and 46 (1972) Each is then followed by my 'translation' according to the Rule of Three as promoted here.

A 'The biological organism corresponds to the function of adaptation: in the sense that it mediates relations with the physical world, adapting to it, manipulating it or transforming it. It is through the organism that the system both adapts to the environment and adapts the environment to its needs.'. In the Rule of Three this roughly translates as the generic 'plan' parameter.

G 'The personality corresponds to the function of goal attainment. It is within and through the personality system that objectives are defined, and resources and energy mobilised for the attainment of the desired goals.' Assembly and performance thinking regards this function as being performed by the quasi-mind of the group, so it is not one of the three plan > execute > review > repeat functions. Instead it presides over the whole set of these functions or parameters promoting its purpose like the conductor of an orchestra, in response to the perceived threat or opportunity which caused the group to assemble in the first place. These threats or opportunities in turn are about one or more of the three universal life imperatives: to metabolise energy, self-protect and breed.

I 'The social system represents the function of integration. It is this which creates solidarity, generates loyalties, defines the limits of permissible action and imposes constraints.' According to assembly and performance thinking, this function amounts to the achievement of assembly; in other words, it promotes the assembly of selfish individuals into altruistic cogs in a labour-divided purposeful group.

L 'Culture represents the function of latency or pattern-maintenance. It supplies actors with motivation and support for their actions, by means of the norms, ideals, values and ideologies which it makes available or even imposes upon them.' Parsons's pattern variables are structures that are always changing but always the same. The universality of committee procedures as specified in Robert's Rules of Order (see page 136) is a good example of the persistent emergence of 'pattern variables.' According to the Rule of Three this persistent function is performed in three ways:

1. Motivation and support comes from the presiding quasi-mind already referred to.

2. norms, ideals, values and ideologies are supplied by 'review'; the culture-compiling parameter of the Rule of Three; and

3. The pattern-maintenance described in AGIL is supplied by the iteration of the Rule of Three.

This set of three generic parameters, plan, act and review, is described here as exerting a rational but weak force. It is a force which confers a competitive advantage on those groups which best conform to it over the long term. This 'pattern' of performance can be overpowered by the irrationality of emotion, but emotion soon blows over and, when it does, the surviving people are ready for reassembly. Recovery after a major terrorist bombing is a good example of rationality re-imposing itself. Furthermore, Parsons's idea of differentiation and integration, which builds up multiple groups and arranges them into hierarchies, is easily accommodated in the Rule of Three as the spawning of mini groups. This happens when one element of society – media or law for example – grows and subdivides into subsidiaries.

Kurt Lewin was twelve years older than Parsons and both worked in North American universities. Apparently, they had little useful contact. Parsons's AGIL scheme describing the mechanisms at work in groups was a similar species of theory to Lewin's Spiral already described above. But unlike Lewin, Parsons intended his scheme to apply, as a universal monolith, right up and down the whole hierarchy of society. I believe that satisfied his 'homo economicus type' wish for a fully scientific explanation of society. As I have already said in PART 1 regarding reality from the student's angle, the main reason why Parsons's scheme failed is because it required groups to have their aims set externally; they could not be self-motivating.

9. THE RULE OF THREE EXERTS A WEAK BUT PERSISTENT FORCE REFERRED TO BY TALCOTT PARSONS AS 'PATTERN VARIABLES'

In comparison with the excitement and surging power of emotion, the Rule of Three only exerts a weak force. But unlike emotion it persists during normal times and the group that most consistently respects the Rule of Three in its performance over the long term will thereby gain a competitive advantage. The tortoise beats the hare; in a river-basin it's the regular average flow of water that erodes the valley, not the flash floods. Talcott Parsons is famously difficult to understand but I take his concept of 'pattern variables' or 'pattern maintenance' to be very similar to the observation here that the Rule of Three exerts a weak force.

10. THE RULE OF THREE IS NOT A THEORY; MERELY A DESCRIPTION OF PROCESS

As I have already said in the Introduction, the Rule of Three and indeed the whole concept of assembly and performance thinking of which it is part, cannot be proved. But then neither can the doctrine of natural selection. Both are descriptions of process; they explain what has happened but cannot, and make no attempt to, predict what will happen next.

Warning: beware of metaphors

Let's be careful here about the use of metaphors. It is easy to take them too far. Metaphors are no more than linguistic devices to help us to explain tricky concepts. They use images as a welcome break from the tediousness of logic, so they simply serve to elucidate; to get an idea across. And like all metaphors the Rule of Three should not be taken too literally. Its purpose is to promote the rather abstract idea of using three mutually trumping functions to describe how a social unit performs its job; how they fit together so that it can become an engine of performance; a machine.

If it is taken too literally the triangular feedback control loop conjures up the image of a Manxman running along on his three metaphorical legs. In fact, the reality of performance by either an individual or a social unit is more like the progress of a wheel in which it is always and without exception possible to identify three mutually trumping phases. Phases that are fuzzily separated like the colours of the rainbow, and which frequently throw off mini wheels. The more rigid image of a triangle is easier to explain but perhaps unrealistically simple.

Discarding the triangle in favour of a more fuzzily sectored wheel in no way invalidates the basic idea: that all living creatures, be they individuals or social units, and even including plants, perform by cycling, until the day they die, through a three-phase mutually trumping feedback control loop.

Irrationality

In the tradition of Auguste Comte, Emile Durkheim and Talcott Parsons, assembly and performance thinking applies cold logic to the study of how society works. But A&PT cannot claim to be a full explanation of the wheels of society unless it can accommodate irrationality – the force that can occasionally overwhelm any group from a small business to a nation. We saw that happen during the 2020 worldwide coronavirus epidemic.

Part 2 Interplay Triggered by Emotion comes next. It completes the picture by introducing emotion into the mix. Emotion can beat the group's will to power. Tough luck Nietzsche!

PART 2

SOCIAL THEORY INTERPLAY TRIGGERED BY EMOTION

INTERPLAY
TRIGGERED BY EMOTION

The murmurations of starlings and the shoalings of fish are fascinating to watch. Why do they do it? How do they achieve it? Scientific research has concentrated on experiments about how each individual can sense where its nearest neighbours are at all times; because there lies the secret of how they do it. As to the question of what they have achieved by evolving the ability to do it, well that seems fairly simple; it's explained statistically as the reduction of any one individual's risk of being picked off by a predator.

At least, so say the biologists, but I have never been quite satisfied with that. I think the full explanation may lie in the explosiveness of last-minute panic, rather than in some statistical calculation. It seems more likely that natural selection has developed a sort of social bomb which can explode when death seems imminent. Nature seems to have harnessed the power of social emotion to confuse the enemy. If so, this amounts to the discovery of a behavioural niche; yet another of nature's clever tricks.

In fishing villages, you can sometimes see small fry messing about under the pier, going about in shoals, all pointing the same way. Drop a pebble in and they scatter like lightening, then if you leave them alone, they soon reassemble. It is clearly an instinctive response to danger; you can never catch them with a net. They sometimes scatter even when nothing at all seems to have happened, as though practising a fire-drill. It is a delightful display of the power and the function of emotion used by an assembled social group.

Solitary creatures may use adrenaline, but they cannot harness the explosive potential of social emotion.

A quick flip through macro theory in sociology textbooks turns up little on the role played by emotion in human society. And yet moods such as panic, fear, triumph, shame and disgust play a big part in the workings of the group quasi-mind; they are its accelerators and brake pedals.

The Rule of Three is all very logical and rational, but, as was clear in both the Mother's and Senior Citizen's Tales, emotion plays a major part in real life. A group's quasi-mind deals in primitive moods and emotions which can have a powerful effect on group behaviour. This means that any attempt to understand how society actually works must be able to explain the interplay between the rational behaviour of a group iterating the Rule of Three, and the irrational, or intuitive, behaviour triggered by emotion. Irrationality rules when, as in the scattering of small fry, the discipline of a tribe or military platoon is overcome by hysteria.

This interplay is central in the mechanism of social behaviour. It consists of the give and take between the weak but persistent social force of the Rule of Three, and the destructive, and violent, but temporary, force of emotion. Emotion occasionally has the power to disrupt performance, forcing complete group breakdown. Reassembly then depends on whether a quorum still exists.

Emile Durkheim's three causes of social breakdown: 'anomie', 'forced', and 'another . . .' (he called them 'abnormal forms'), will be described shortly. They powerfully affirm this observation.

The exact same mechanisms also operate on larger social units over longer time periods. For example, this interplay, between assembly and performance, is neatly illustrated in the task, described in The Senior Citizen's Tale, of a football manager. The better his team performs the more money he has to assemble a winning team; the worse, and he begins to struggle. Vicarious spectator emotion is a powerful catalyst at several levels of the process. These assembly and performance dynamics are at play between world-famous teams every week in every national football league. These mechanisms can help us to understand the sometimes-bewildering interactions of self-motivated social groups including football teams, government departments, multinational corporations and criminal gangs. These mechanisms show how our social building-blocks are continually sorting themselves out in the rough-and-tumble hierarchy we call society. Importantly they show where the irrational, annoyingly unquantifiable and unpredictable power of social emotion fits in the mix.

Groups Go Through Life Cycles

Human social groups go through life cycles. Ancient Rome was once a small village. They start as teams and can grow into multinational corporations, but all must eventually decline and die. This is just as true for local building firms as it is for nation states.

In a vigorous young group, when any one of the plan > act > review jobs has become too big for a handful of individuals, new recruits are taken on and, bingo! a new mini group is spawned, which is to say recruited and 'assembled'. However small, this becomes a cooperating group in its own right.

The purpose of a new mini group, the jobs into which its labour should be divided and the architecture and parameters of its 'business model' are as usual best decided during assembly. I have first-hand experience of this. As a young man I once got a job at Unilever, the huge multinational food conglomerate. The job was in a newly formed consulting department, a new mini group. But unfortunately for me, though I didn't understand it at the time, the purpose of the department was fundamentally unclear to all concerned; my boss was weak; and not possessing the skilful consultant's ability to cope with ambiguity, I got the sack for trying to clarify it.

Normally a vigorous young group takes structural expansion in its stride. But, as Anthony King demonstrated in *Boat Race: Rhythm and the Possibility of Collective Performance* (2011), success may depend on flexibility in response to events. Dissent within a crew can flash back and forth emotionally between, on the one hand, beneficial correction-in-performance and, on the other, damaging rebellion and consequent reassembly. It is often difficult for the bystander, some-times even the coach, to disentangle the quick-fire interplay between assembly and performance.

Groups, Like Raindrops, Appear, Grow, Merge and Collapse

Society consists of distinct groups, each a social unit iterating its own particular control loop. They are constantly forming, overlapping, interfering with each other, merging and disintegrating. The whole picture is like raindrop rings forming in ultra-slow motion on the surface of a pond. This illustrates the ever moving and bewildering raw material; the rough-and-tumble of society which a sociologist has to deal with.

In *The Division of Labour* (1902), Emile Durkheim recognised that every social group is a mini society in its own right and is integrated into the overall social hierarchy. While commenting on Emile Durkheim's observations, C. Calhoun says:

> We know in fact that societies are formed by a certain number of segments of unequal size that overlap one another. These moulds are not artificial creations, particularly in the beginning. Even when they have become conventional, they imitate and reproduce so far as possible the forms of natural arrangement that preceded them. Many ancient societies are maintained in this form. The largest among these sub-divisions, those that include the others, correspond to the nearest social type. Likewise, among the segments of which they in turn are made up, the most extensive are the remains of the type that comes directly below the preceding one and so on. Among the most advanced peoples we find traces of the most primitive organisation.
>
> *Classical Sociological Theory* (2002), page 143

We routinely use the nation state as the unit of study but we pay less attention to how Durkheim's internal groups – opportunistic street gangs, earnest charities, families and tribes, rowing clubs, ruthless political parties and multinational corporations – coexist in this rough-and-tumble nested hierarchy to make up a usually, more or less, harmonious society.

People are constantly sensing the social electricity, the emotion, pulsing through the hierarchy they live in. In a catastrophic event such as an earthquake, fire, flood, declaration of war or outbreak of plague, social electricity has the power to dissolve the boundaries in this hierarchy; it can amalgamate small groups into bigger alliances to deal with a problem.

Some groups are ephemeral, a working party may disband a few hours after formation, whereas Ancient Egypt endured for many centuries. Eventually each must decay and vanish, but at any one time they, together, are what society consists of. The raindrop rings metaphor illustrates separate but interconnected performing groups and their occasional amalgamations. When the social electricity of a major disturbance eventually subsides, the boring old previous boundaries in the hierarchy are usually restored, sometimes with structural adjustments. This is homeostasis at work. The 1999 Turkish earthquake referred to in PART 3 below and the 1980s' Margaret Thatcher privatisations described above in The Employee's Tale, provide examples of homeostasis.

Social Breakdown Caused by Reverse Trumping

If the Rule of Three is valid then all cases of social breakdown can be attributed to reverse trumping. Furthermore, each type of breakdown – there are three of them – is accompanied or lubricated by emotion.

If, as argued above, there can be no more and no fewer than three mutually trumping social performance parameters: Plan > act > review, then logically there can be no more and no fewer than three reverse trumping categories to match them. And each category gums up the works. They can be called: rebellion, autocracy and sclerosis.

Rebellion. The French Revolution was a spectacular example of rebellion: citizens in planning mode reversed into and smashed review mode or culture as embodied in the law. Things got out of hand and the loop went into reverse; civic life was disrupted and was not properly reassembled for about ten years.

Autocracy. In dictatorships, as in Russia under Stalin, act reverses into and silences planning, stifling the media and freedom of speech. In the long run this eventually diminishes the group's creative ability, weakening its performance in competition with more democratic rival corporations or nations.

Sclerosis. This happens when review or culture mode becomes too powerful, too bureaucratic, thus inhibiting executive leadership. The decay of great civilisations such as Ancient Egypt, China, Maya and Rome can be attributed to blockages in loop iteration at the culture-compiling phase; they failed to move with the times and went into terminal decline.

While researching for this book, I was thrilled to discover that over one hundred years ago Emile Durkheim promoted essentially the same thing. At the end of his classic work on the division of labour, Durkheim referred to the 'abnormal forms of the division of labour.' He said there are three categories of these abnormal forms, or failures, of social cohesion. He called them 'The Anomic Division of Labour': *my rebellion*; 'The Forced Division of Labour': *my dictatorship*; and 'Another Anomic Form': *my sclerosis*. See Emile Durkheim, op.cit., Book 3.

The main difference between Durkheim's ideas and the assembly and performance thinking proposed here is that Durkheim did not notice that a cybernetic feedback control loop describes social performance. The application of cybernetics to the study of social dynamics was only later promoted by Norbert Weiner and Talcott Parsons. Furthermore, Durkheim did not describe the *a priori* continuum of social mechanisms from microbes to humans which underpins the assembly and performance thinking promoted here.

Assembly, Performance and Emotion Summarised

Assembly and performance thinking describes two quite distinct perceptions, and it shows how emotion provokes the interplay between them.

Assembly thinking draws on Darwinian natural selection. It reviews the latest scholarship about the way in which social creatures have been able to evolve from the default solitary condition despite Darwin's 'struggle for existence'. It recognises that cooperation can be evolutionarily stable if the social group can become a unit of natural selection: Brave man dies so that group can survive.

Performance is quite different. Assuming a group of individuals has assembled to do something, the question then is: 'OK, so how does it go about its business – how does it perform?' The functions of life subdivide into energy acquisition, self-protection and reproduction. Solitaries do these by trial and error or more accurately: plan > execute > review > repeat. It's a continually iterating process or 'cybernetic feedback control loop'. The argument is that the logic of group performance is exactly the same as that of solitary performance; this logic is even obeyed by cooperating microbes. In cooperating mammals, the loop can be epitomised as plan (as a group) > act (as a group) > review (as a group) > and repeat. These parameters are mutually trumping as in the game scissors, paper and stone.

The selection of three specific parameters for any performance and the order of their trumping is an assembly, not a performance, requirement.

Only two instructions are necessary to set up this rule of three:

1. the three most effective parameters must be identified, during assembly, and, 2. the order of their trumping must be agreed, again, during assembly, and adhered to. It is a beautifully simple arrangement.

So, assembly and performance thinking consists of these two quite distinct arguments. Furthermore, they are plainly integral in any explanation of how society works. It seems that during millennia of hubris or self-important thinking, they have been wrongly put together and that this mistake has been deeply embedded in the folklores, religions and cultures of the world. Hubris must be side-stepped before the mechanisms of assembly and performance and the emotionally charged interplay between them can be got at. Otherwise the different elements of human social behaviour are simply too interwoven, too entangled in philosophy, myth and religious dogma, for us to recognise them. We had to discard the idea that the sun goes around the earth before we could understand how the solar system works.

Emotion, far from being an irrational nuisance, breathes the realities of life into the dynamics of our social mechanisms. Rich arrays of social insight can unfold after one has noticed the difference between assembly and performance, and the way in which emotion lubricates their interplay. These insights are surveyed in PART 3 – Illuminations.

PART 3

ILLUMINATIONS

Common Origin

Several aspects of our social behaviour can be illuminated by thinking in terms of assembly and performance and by the way in which their interplay is provoked by emotion. One or two of these insights are chillingly bleak, others are optimistic. Their common origin may add a ring of truth to assembly and performance thinking.

Bullying Is Ugly, but Natural; It Should Be Controlled by Emotional Disgust

Bullying is not a neutral word. Typified by the music-hall drill-sergeant, it draws attention to its own unpleasantness. Its animal function is essentially the correcting of awkward team members. This description explains why it can't be eradicated and why attempts to do so are utopian. Bullying is a social mechanism which is closely related to cheater-detection. One can imagine a tribe in which bullying has been completely eradicated. Without drill-sergeants it would be less disciplined, less effective in competition, than those in which uncooperative members are bullied into conformity. The brake here is that bullying can so easily arouse *collective* emotions of disgust in humans. This response is surely a social trait, evolved to prevent excessive bullying.

So here we have another reason for being grateful for the irrational power of emotion. Once again it comes to the rescue as a sort of safety-valve which breaks up behaviour that might harm the functioning of the group. An over-disciplined group, ancient Sparta for example, may win the war, but it will lose out in the long run.

Assembly and performance thinking recommends that the way to control excessive bullying is to enlist, or harness, the social power of this emotional disgust.

Morality: A Language-Like Propensity to Accept Tribal Rules for Self-Restraint

Emile Durkheim said in *The Division of Labour in Society*, op.cit., that 'morality consists in the set of conditions that make social solidarity possible'. Here I define morality as a language-like propensity to accept tribal rules for self-restraint, which amounts to much the same thing.

Morality dazzles us, it is a motivator which can make us do counter-intuitive, altruistic things. But assembly and performance thinking reveal it to be an unreliable philosophical concept.

Its function, closely allied to cheater-detection and the flipside of bullying, is to support teamwork by overcoming selfishness. It is best understood as the word we use to explain the collective psychological enforcer of a tribe's adopted code of social behaviour. An infinite number of moral codes is possible but there cannot be an eternally right one. These codes are culturally evolved, adapted and taught.

Morality is an introspective, subjective concept. It is a non-thing, a mental construct. It vanishes when the human interpreting intellect is absent (see PART 1, The Mother's Tale, above) so its pursuit leads, like the mythical Oozlum bird, to whirlpools of insoluble debate. But a definition of this elusive non-thing is necessary, and my best 'long-form'

224

effort is that morality is: 'the word we use for a genetically inherited, optional, self-restraining propensity to learn, obey and teach tribal rules which, by overcoming selfishness, supports altruistic teamwork.'

Optional here refers to the ability to cooperate or split as appropriate, see PART 2, and the genetic inheritance in this definition is an evolved language-like nature/nurture propensity.

This self-restraining motivator, 'morality' for want of a better word, is an essential function of assembly. It is at work in all cooperating mammals.

But there's more to it than that because, though it must operate in teamwork, and can even lead to personal death, this small still voice of conscience must be silenced in the workings of the group's quasi-mind. If a mammal tribe were reprogrammed to maintain its altruistic self-restraint in its external affairs it would quickly become extinct. This was Machiavelli's famous insight in *The Prince* (1532). When group survival is at stake, he said, leaders who allow morality to guide their foreign policy should be deposed to prevent group failure.

Furthermore, in solitaries, at the other extreme of the behavioural spectrum, morality would also be a pointless hindrance. Altruistic solitaries: turtles, snakes, fish or polar bears would quickly become extinct.

In public debate moral weakness is often eloquently lamented. Recent examples include our failure to stand up against the criticism of Jews, and discrimination against ethnic and sexual minorities. These debates usually ignore the genetically embedded mechanisms of cooperation which are explained in assembly and performance thinking. If we want to control the nasty aspects of our animal nature it is wiser to recognise than to deny them; lamentation only has a short reach. It's better to understand the devil than to pretend he isn't there.

Assembly and performance thinking explains moral behaviour biologically. It is seen as neither good nor bad; rather as a vital mechanism without which the social mammal would quickly go extinct.

Group Ruthlessness Is Vital to Species Survival: Message for Schoolchildren

Ruthlessness towards the outside world is a universal attribute of group behaviour. When threatened, even charities are ultimately indifferent to outsiders, not to mention those perennial baddies: church, temple, mosque and synagogue. In terrorism, infuriation by an external agent provokes the assembly of a fighting force. A similar process assembles inner-city hooligan gangs, with their emblems, rules, quasi-minds and their private slang dialects. These gangs can arise irrespective of class or status; for example, until recently high-court judges, senior doctors and clergymen paraded proudly amongst the Protestants in the Northern Irish sectarian marches. As these prominent citizens switched modes their individuality became absorbed into their role as cogs-in-a-group. This mode-switching phenomenon explains that, vile though it was, Hitler's Nazism was classic human behaviour. Many similar atrocities have occurred before and since Hitler. The mechanisms of assembly suggest that the prevention of inhuman behaviour must concentrate on resolving the reason for the infuriation.

Assembly and performance thinking says that not just some but without exception all cooperating groups are ruthlessly indifferent to the outside world when pursuing their corporate interests. They readily obey the law but only to the extent that legal punishments would damage their group's survival and prosperity. In this respect the law is readily accepted by the group as just another external factor or condition. Group ruthlessness is well understood in academic sociology. The point here is just that the simple way in which assembly and performance thinking illuminates the problem of group ruthlessness adds to its plausibility.

These observations are not put forward as proposals; they merely show why group ruthlessness is central in the mechanism of human social behaviour. It cannot be eradicated. We include sex education in today's school curriculum, but it is arguably more important for the health of society that youngsters should be taught formally about the integrated mechanisms of social behaviour. Youngsters deserve to be given formal lessons on how social assembly, when combined with the Rule of Three and when stimulated by emotion, can trigger some of the nastier facts of life. These include playground bullying, criminal gang behaviour, corporate greed, terrorism, warfare and genocide.

Corporate Greed Is a Simple Case of Group Ruthlessness

Corporate greed is a sub-heading under the ruthlessness of groups. It is unpleasant but it cannot be eliminated by moral obligation. The hope that voluntary codes of behaviour can control the biggest multinationals and banks, or even the small ones, is demonstrated here as wishful thinking: utopian pie in the sky. This naivety reached its apogee in the 1980s when the privatisations by Margaret Thatcher and Ronald Reagan and their famous Big Bang deregulations opened the floodgates to corporate greed. Moral obligation or the small still voice of conscience only operates within a group, never between it and the outside world.

Banking scandals, excessive pay levels and monopolistic price-rigging are worldwide demonstrations of the inability of moral obligation to control group behaviour. Prevention must be externally imposed through adverse publicity and effective law. Because they must be effective, legal sanctions on corporate greed should include fines and jail sentences which do real damage to the actual corporation, not necessarily to any one individual.

From bacteria via ants and rats to humans, there is no intrinsic curb to the harmful excesses of group ambition. In humans, corporate greed must be prevented by law. Such curbs on group behaviour must be applied by external agents.

Victor Frankl's 'Urge to Meaning'

Victor Frankl's urge to meaning is often referred to as the third Viennese school, after Sigmund Freud's urge to happiness and Alfred Adler's urge to power. Frankl's appalling experiences as a prisoner in Nazi concentration camps convinced him that having a strong meaning in one's life was the ultimate thing which prevented fellow prisoners from giving up hope and dying. After his release Frankl developed this perception into the theory of psychiatric Logotherapy which is practised worldwide today. His book, *Man's Search for Meaning*, has to date sold sixteen million copies.

In his description of Logotherapy, Frankl says:

> By declaring that man is responsible and must actualise the potential meaning of his life, I wish to stress that the true

> meaning of life is to be discovered in the world rather than within man or his own psyche, as though it were a closed system.

It seems clear that by 'in the world' Frankl mainly meant 'in society'. The Rule of Three offers a practical description of how actually 'society' works, a description of its dynamics. And since logotherapists recommend that we should find the meaning of life *in society* this enrichment may be useful to them. If so, that would be another illumination shone by A&PT.

In Frankl's day (1905–1997) it was acceptable to work with a simple idea. Society was one of those 'we all know what we mean' concepts, a sort of self-governing country in which people moved about like ants in robust harmony. Since the dawn of history society has consisted of men and women, farmers, seafarers, traders and factory workers: of leaders, thinkers, teachers, storytellers, manufacturers, children, adults and old folk. But it can be difficult for an outsider to find a place in society. Frankl recognised that many psychological problems are due to this dilemma. His solution, known as Logo-therapy, would help people to find a meaning in life. It was brilliant. But the Assembly and Performance Thinking promoted here with its Rule of Three suggests that a more precise understanding of the working parts, the dynamics, of society could now be available. I am suggesting that this thinking could add considerable effectiveness to the clinical practice of Logotherapy.

The Rule of Three depicts society as a sort of dartboard divided into three sectors: plan, act and review. People can then be asked, in therapy, to place themselves with an imaginary dart on the board according to their beliefs about their own skills and inclinations. Some believing themselves to want to be action men or women; others more concerned with culture, the law, or again with deciding what's to be done. Those who feel unsure where to place the dart could put it further out from the bullseye, while those who are confident about themselves would go nearer to the centre.

This is of course only a descriptive device, and it may be more helpful if instead of a dartboard we think of a wheel with spokes. There would be twelve spokes: four depicting various planning functions, debating, politicking, simulating, etc.; four spokes for types of action, such as strategizing, managing, policing, etc., and four spokes for reviewing such as recording, adjusting the law and fixing cultural tramlines.

The will to meaning is illustrated in these imaginary diagrams by a person's desire to move closer to the bullseye or the hub. The contention here being that the closer you can get to the centre the greater the meaning in your life – the less likely that you are prone to die in an appalling situation like the Gulag. So, for example, planners when closest to the centre will have more contact with and a better understanding of those in the other sectors; the action -brigade and the scribes; they will have better working relationships. This reinforces Frankl's will to meaning; it encourages the wish to move closer to the centre.

I am no therapist, more like the fool who rushes in where angels fear to tread, but it may be worth noting here that Frankl's 'will to meaning' shares this centralising motive with Alfred Adler's 'will to power', but not Sigmund Freud's 'will to happiness'. Adler's 'individual psychology' might also be enriched by Assembly and Performance thinking and particularly by the Rule of Three.

And what about the women? Throughout his book Frankl uses the gender-neutral convention of his day which tacitly included women under 'men', as in 'mankind' for example. This is unfortunate because existential frustration has always been more common in boys and men than in girls and women; by their very gender most women have always had clearer meanings in their lives than men. Frankl's indifference to this is obvious; his writings are all men, men, men. To modern readers it can seem perverse. But as described in PART 1 above, the mother wisely tolerates her man's pomposity because she knows he will be the first to get killed defending his family in a war.

The Law: Separating Individual from Group Law

It follows from the arguments above about morality, group ruthlessness and corporate greed that the task of law-making for individuals differs fundamentally from the task of law-making for groups. We cannot expect to have a satisfactory legal system if we continually confuse the misbehaviour of individuals, who naturally accept moral rules, with the misbehaviour of groups which do not. The costly muddles the law gets itself into have already been mentioned in The Mother's Tale (PART 1 above).

Ignorance of the law is commonplace, if it weren't there'd be no need to establish the dubious legal principle that such ignorance is not a valid defence. The very need to trumpet this principle so loud and clear is a sad acknowledgement that the law is frequently unclear. We might be able to simplify things for legislators, police and offenders if we were to accept the individual versus group distinction in law-making. The drafting of law in Parliament, its interpretation in court and enforcement by the police would in each case be split into two. Individual law would deal with moral codes covering transgressions which undermine teamwork. These are things like murder, theft, deceit, divorce, and so on. Group law would be completely different. It would deal with the anti-social tricks which groups get up to, including corporate tax evasion, financial misreporting, price-fixing, deceitful marketing, corruption, excessive bonuses, pollution, health problems, and habitat destruction. There would be separate courts, judges, magistrates, barristers and jury systems. There would also be quite different punishments and prisons.

Group law would impose daunting and effective fines, prison sentences and permanently damaging shame for corporate bosses. There would also be prison sentences for guilty 'independent' auditors. But the main target of group law would be to punish the transgressing group; not necessarily any individual as such.

This individual versus group distinction is of course accommodated in the laws of all modern democracies, but the need for this accommodation usually creates such haphazard legal patchworks that multitudes of highly trained lawyers are necessary to guide legislators, police, offenders and greedy competitors through the labyrinthine pathways of what ought to be very much simpler systems.

This is another example of the explanatory potential of assembly and performance thinking; it is offered as a thought experiment, not a specific proposal.

Psychiatry Repairs Faults in Personalised Social Response Libraries

According to assembly and performance thinking, Freud was right but unfortunately, he got side-tracked by sex and the subconscious. Assembly and performance thinking puts Freud's ideas back on the main track; his id, ego and super-ego correspond well to the three modes of assembly identified here: solitary, team player and team.

A large part of psychiatry involves the repair of assembly disorders. These are the cases where a child's early socialisation has somehow gone wrong. This occasionally happens in the rough and tumble of family and tribal life. They are the cases where faults have been built into the child's developing social-response habits – see personal library-building and Bourdieu's habitus: PART 2, Cooperate-or-split (p. 162).

The perception that the three assembly modes correspond nicely to Freud's id, ego and super-ego adds credibility to assembly and performance thinking. This works the other way round too: assembly and performance thinking may give students of psychiatry a richer perspective, connecting their profession to the wider mechanisms of society. What I mean is that separating the mechanisms of assembly from those of performance might help to render psychiatry less of a dark art to the general public. It is usually the difficult art of repairing faults in personalised social-response reference libraries.

As Freud pointed out most psychiatric disorders are the result of damage done when socialisation goes wrong in childhood. It seems very possible that if he had followed this promising lead to its conclusion instead of being seduced by sex and the subconscious, he would have hit upon assembly and performance thinking. He was more than halfway there with his id, ego and super-ego.

As well as clarifying pathology for individuals, the distinction between assembly and performance also suggests ways to repair malfunctioning groups like football teams, rowing eights and political parties. This is dealt with next.

Group Pathology: Social Repair Using Assembly and Performance Thinking

Psychiatry aims to repair damage to their 'social response libraries' suffered by children If this can be accepted it may be possible to do similar repair jobs for groups when they get into trouble. I mean that it may be possible to use assembly and performance thinking in a formal practice of group pathology. This would be similar to psychiatry today.

Human social groups go through lifecycles just like individuals: they start as small teams and families and they can grow into nations and multinational corporations, but all must eventually decline until finally they die. This is just as true for nation states as it is for local builders.

In a vigorous young group, when any one of the plan>act> or review jobs has become too big for one individual, others are recruited and, bingo! a new mini group is spawned or assembled. However small, this is a cooperating group in its own right.

A mini group has all the social features and mechanisms described in PART 2. The purpose of a new mini group, the jobs into which its labour should be divided and the architecture and parameters of its 'business model', are best decided during assembly.

Job description and allocation in a newly assembling group is critical. It must be flexible; trial and error, or plan > act > review >, is the very essence of progress and normally a vigorous young group takes structural revision in its stride. But a major reshuffle or disturbance can harness the power of emotion and disrupt *performance*. Anthony King demonstrated in the *British Journal of Sociology* 2011 pp. 565–585 'Boat Race', etc., how success depended on flexibility in response to events. Dissent within a crew flashed back and forth between, on the one hand beneficial correction-in-performance and on the other, damaging rebellion. It is often difficult for the bystander, sometimes even the coach, to disentangle the quick-fire interplay between assembly and performance.

The purpose of a formal 'science' of group pathology would be to advise on breakdown repair and to recommend best practice for its future avoidance. This would offer for conflicted groups what psychiatry offers for conflicted individuals. And a significant part of the job would involve recognising and dealing with the emotion that usually haunts group malfunction. The procedure would be first to identify the plan > execute > review > control loop at work where the group or society seems to be malfunctioning, and then to examine the way in which it has been *assembled*. The aim being to ensure the smooth iteration of the group's feedback control loop in *performance*.

The worldwide management consulting profession does indeed offer an impressive range of group pathology services. Management-consulting firms, journals and business schools comprise a worldwide multibillion-dollar industry, some gurus charging $200,000 a day for their advice. But as the English A-level Business Studies curric-ulum demonstrates (see *AQA Business for A-Level* (2015) by Ian Marcuse and others), there is a wide and occasionally conflicting range of management theories.

Another reason why management consulting falls short of being a true profession of group pathology is that it limits itself to monetarised groups, which only make up part of society. (See above PART 1 The Apprentice's Tale, 'Monetisation'.)

A group-pathology profession, based on assembly and performance thinking, should be able to clarify the confusing and conflicting advice which today bombards our social groups, from small businesses to multinationals, NGOs and government teams to armies and nations. The procedure should be guided by assembly and performance thinking, the aim in every case being to ensure the smooth iteration of the feedback control loop.

Historical Successes of Social Energy Explained as Smooth Loop Iteration

According to assembly and performance thinking, the ideal set-up is where the mutually trumping institutions nested in social hierarchy are harmoniously iterating their navigation loops, planning, acting and reviewing as they go. This comes close to becoming a version of utopia.

In real life we are dealing with blockages and reversals all over the place: autocracy here, sloth or corruption there, rebellion simmering elsewhere. But every so often humans have put on a spectacular surge of creativity. Examples include Ancient Egypt, Athens under Pericles in the fifth century BC, Ancient China, the Roman republic, the Mayans and Renaissance Florence. In these cases lucky coincidences did indeed provide the rich resources, favourable geography and gifted leaders which sparked success; yes OK, but luck cannot have been the full explanation for their longevity, and it seems possible that in each case the navigation control loops of the main nested institutions were iterating more efficiently than usual in these societies. Studies along these lines might open a fruitful line of enquiry for historians and might give pause for thought to politicians.

Hegel's Dialectic Less Realistic than the Spiralling Loop?

The concept that society progresses by a succession of swings between extreme positions is attributed mainly to Georg Hegel. It was then famously claimed by Karl Marx to describe an inevitable path to an ideal form of permanent socialism. But that has not happened, and the dialectic is today a somewhat vague and discredited idea, occasionally useful to sociologists and historians.

It may be more useful to think of human history as society progressing through the plan > execute > review iterations of the control loop. In these spiralling iterations, culture adjusts continually as it incorporates successive waves of technology from steam via petrol and nuclear energy to the electronic age. Kurt Lewin's progressive spirals have already been referred to in PART 2 above. This control loop argument is put forward here as a more realistic way of writing history than Hegel's dialectic.

Terrorism and Rogue Nations

Terrorist groups are notoriously difficult to defeat. In Greek mythology the Hydra epitomised what today we call a terrorist organisation; it was a fierce monster with many heads and if you managed to chop one off, two would grow in its place Assembly and performance thinking suggests that the way to kill off a criminal gang, terrorist organisation or rogue nation is to encourage reverse trumping in its ranks. That's to say to disrupt the iteration of its feedback control loop by encouraging rebellion, dictatorship or sclerosis. In all these solutions the key is to weaken the rogue leadership's popular support. In other words, to weaken its quasi-mind.

Direct policing or military intervention merely heightens the social electricity and popular support available to the rogue leadership. The reverse trumping strategies seek to exploit the three types of group malfunction already described above. These strategies have long been understood and used, but a clear understanding of the mechanisms of society would probably ease their implementation. This perception would be especially useful in public debate at all social levels: local pub, Parliament, and among the chattering class. And it would emphasise the folly of military intervention.

To those who may think these views seem right-wing, I would reply that assembly and performance thinking will probably irritate people both on the right and the left in equal proportions.

Video-Gaming Addiction

Video-gaming addiction is referred to in the senior citizen's tale in PART 1 above. It just remains to be repeated here that assembly and performance thinking illuminates, or highlights, the interplay between assembling a team and its performance. Video gaming also demonstrates the two opposing types of motivation: 1. the rationality of the Rule of Three, which is a weak but persistent force and 2. the strong but ephemeral force of emotion. Emotion is seen here as a sort of fire-alarm or safety-valve which can disrupt performance, triggering a complete reassembly and repurposing of the new group's quasi-mind

The illumination here is about why gaming is so addictive. The answer is that it accurately simulates the social thrills and spills of inter-group competition or 'gang warfare' which the youngster navigates in real life. Video gaming very accurately simulates the quasi-mind motivators and performance trade-offs that regulate our daily lives. And come to think of it, apart perhaps from sex, there is little that is more important to our survival and prosperity than the performance of the groups we belong to. We depend on them. No wonder our youngsters are hooked.

Self-Motivating Robots Are Impossible: They Have No Ambition

The claim that through the workings of their already-assembled quasi-minds, social groups are self-motivating comes up again and again throughout this book. This enables us to make a clear distinction between robots which depend on outside agents to motivate them and social groups which do not. This means that until scientists can create the will or ambition which is built into all life forms, until they can create life, *it will always be impossible to create self-motivating robots.*

Advice to robot designers trying to create self-motivating robots:

'You can't do it! If ambition or will is the elusive essence, the soul, which must be endowed on inert matter to make it alive, it follows that until life can be created ambition must always be set by an external agent and the robot will always trend to a pre-set homeostatic zero. Until you have learnt how to endow inert matter with the ambition to metabolise, self-protect and breed you will not be able to create the quasi-minds necessary for self-motivated robots. Until then they are science fiction, mere loose talk. And "emergence" cannot side-step this impossibility.'

Looting Happens Naturally in a Sudden Social-Electricity Power Cut

Looting happens in a sudden social-electricity power cut. Assembly, which has to be positively maintained all the time because the default condition is solitary, collapses in a social-electricity power cut; the group dissolves, we all revert to solitary mode, and it's every man for himself. This explanation from the mechanisms of assembly may be the best way to understand and deal with looting. It also reflects credibility back onto assembly and performance thinking.

The Balance of Powers Should Be Media > Executive > Law > Media >

The classic triumvirate of powers: legislature, executive and judiciary, in which any two are supposed to combine to control the third, is attributed to de Montesquieu's *De L'Esprit des Lois*, published 1748 (Morris,1969). The idea has inspired many of the national constitutions in use today, for example in the USA and France. But in practice the executive, because it offers the most glamorous careers, attracts the most talented youngsters, so demagogues regularly ride roughshod over the combined powers of legislature and judiciary, censoring the media, interfering with the law and sometimes leading to unrest and even rebellion.

Because the American and French systems are not mutually trumping, they are not closed loops, and this is a serious weakness; it is sometimes easy for the executive to divide and conquer. In America, for example, it simply means setting Congress, the legislature, against the Supreme Court.

The only institution that can really frighten the executive is public opinion, typically expressed by the media. The Rule of Three, claims to explain how groups perform. It implies that the three-phase mutual trumping loop should be formally built into all national constitutions. In such a system the institutions of state should be equivalents for media, which trumps the executive, the executive which acts and enforces the law, and the law which controls the media. Each of these three functions or parameters has several guises. Media represents 'review' or gossip, the executive represents 'act' or coercive power, and the law represents 'learn' or culture.

Why Did Turkey and Greece Temporarily Suspend Hostilities for an Earthquake?

Old enemies Greece and Turkey cooperated wholeheartedly to deal with the tragedy of the 1999 Turkish earthquake. But sadly, the truce did not last. The dynamics of group assembly and performance explain why this was entirely predictable. Emotion had swept the rational historical antagonism aside. Group boundaries were dissolved and both sides worked together in humanitarian relief work. But emotion though a strong force is short lived (see PART 2 The Interplay Between Assembly and Performance), and when the crisis subsided, public opinion ensured that the old, persistent, weak force of rationality was restored. The traditional boundaries were reassembled, and hostilities resumed.

These dynamics also explain the naivety of the many 1980s' industrial privatisations in the UK, the USA, and other industrialised nations. Here the business model of fiercely competitive corporate efficiency was expected to eliminate the problems of laziness and public apathy. Some hope! The intended competitive set-up was predictably artificial. This allowed the top dogs and smart operators of industry to borrow money and cream off the assets without having to deliver their vague promises. It was argued that a shake-up of many cosy traditional industrial practices was beneficial, but the pain was inhuman, and It was a bonanza of corporate greed.

These two examples demonstrate how the bad old ways can effortlessly re-establish themselves after a social disturbance. They also hint at how it might have been possible to avoid many problems if only we had had a better understanding of the mechanism of society. Machiavelli pointed out group amorality in 1532.

Social dynamics can move extremely fast and when they do, it can be difficult to distinguish what's actually happening. The boat-race example mentioned above shows how the plan > act > review > functions can sometimes seem to overlap and collide. These observations about mini-group formation, and about the difference between revision-in-progress and reversal-with-reassembly, may help to disentangle the sometimes bewildering interplay between factions in social dynamics. The interactions can be lightning quick making it almost impossible to follow what's going on; or they can be almost imperceptibly slow.

Group successes and failures have always been intuitively understood of course, especially in retrospect, and in history writing. It must be recognised that in some cases of group malfunction a definitive explanation of what actually went wrong may never be possible. But assembly and performance thinking might help the participants to nip social malfunction in the bud by developing a practice of group pathology. This would do for social groups what psychiatry does today for individuals.

Maybe, if instead of his balance of powers, de Montesquieu had proposed the Rule of Three, then the French Revolution might have been averted. As it happened, popular opinion representing the 'plan' function in the Rule of Three, mobilising the power of emotion, reverse-trumped into and overwhelmed the law. The overwhelming of law perfectly describes what happened in the French Revolution; 'anomie' as Emile Durkheim called it.

The 2020 World Covid 19 Epidemic

As I write this the Coronavirus epidemic, Covid 19, is affecting human populations all over the planet. Though devastating and deadly to certain senior citizens, it seems to be temporary. It is expected that as in earlier flu outbreaks, an antidote will be found, and the virus will be under control within a year or two. Its course illustrates the power of emotion, but it does not alter the basic arguments of assembly and performance thinking in any way. It confirms them.

Bureaucracy Is Uniquely Human

Bureaucracy which enables separated groups to combine into one coordinated enterprise, can be defined as super-assembly. This shows bureaucracy to be a unique and powerful human achievement. It seems only humans have evolved the ability to use written language to integrate the activities of separate groups. The Roman Empire was one example, another is in today's multinational corporations. The invention of bureaucracy through advanced communication is probably the one thing that truly sets humans apart from all other animals.

This is another illumination attributable to assembly and performance thinking. The social insects have developed caste systems which greatly enhances their cooperation, whereas the mammals including humans mainly use brainpower. But the ability in a social animal to coordinate separated cooperating groups for a common purpose seems to be uniquely human.

We use writing for this, but writing may not be the only possible way to communicate between groups separated by the inability to see, hear, smell, taste and touch each other. There does not seem to be any reason why life forms could not one day evolve the use of electromagnetism, radio waves or quantum mechanics to communicate across separation gaps. Ants could use such waves to warn about danger perhaps, or sperm whales could use their bulbous heads to compare feeding-grounds.

Our bureaucratic ability to co-ordinate separated teams has greatly eased our lives but it has also given us a frightening power over nature. The genie, now much enhanced by the internet, has got out of the bottle – but can we control it?

Culture Is a Tramline System

Culture in social mammals can be characterised as: 'Look, this is how we do things around here.' Culture needs to be flexible enough to move with the times but rigid enough to serve as a coordinating force whose tramlines prevent chaos during performance. We should drive on the same side of the road, use the same financial conventions and speak the same language. Galileo felt the power of culture in 1633 when the Catholic Church found him guilty of blasphemy. Culture opposes innovation or, more accurately, culture specifies the conventions to be respected by innovators. Natural selection operates here to ensure that while there is an infinity of possible cultures, or ways of laying out social tramlines, only those most appropriate for tribal survival and prosperity are selected. Darwin pointed this out in *The Descent of Man*, and in *Darwin's Cathedral* (2002), D. S. Wilson reinforced it using religion as his example.

As has already been noted at the beginning of PART 2 above, cultural adaptation may have taken over from speciation in human evolution. Culture in a mammal tribe is a set of best methods or rules passed down through successive generations. These 'know-how' skills are ways of adapting to local circumstances. Humans have made enormous strides in inter-communication during the last five thousand years. This is largely due to the invention of reading and writing. It was then a small step to use this invention to accelerate the accumulations of best local cultures. These largely enshrine tribal knowledge about the best ways to do things in specific circumstances.

Local cultural adaptations in social mammals including elephants, orcas and chimpanzees have been illustrated in many recent TV wildlife programmes, and it is suggested that, as Herbert Spencer said (see PART 1 above) in humans at least, cultural adaptation may have superseded speciation. In other words, it is suggested that the written spread of 'know-how' or technology may be the main reason why distinct *sub-species* of earlier humans no longer *recognisably* exist, as they once did when the Neanderthals and Denisovans were around. Modern humans, bearing mixtures of these earlier genes, have been able, it is said, by using advanced communication and written records, to adapt to such diverse habitats as tropical rainforest, arctic tundra, desert, high mountain, seaside and river valley. It does not seem too far-fetched to speculate that, if they had been deprived of the ability to write, and were then left alone to go their own separate ways for another seventy thousand years, the ancient Tibetans and the Incas might by now have evolved into separate species of Homo unable to breed together.

Culture represents the 'review' function in the 'plan > act > review >' control loop. If a tribe's culture is too rigid, it can reverse into 'act' causing stagnation, but if it is too flexible, it may fail to prevent 'plan' from breaking the rules and thus invite chaos and rebellion. Culture is further examined under God below, but first a word about valuing art.

Art: The Froth at the Cutting Edge of Culture Sets the Scene

Paintings, songs, music, sculpture, books, architecture, catch-phrases, graffiti, dirty jokes and fairy-stories are cultural artefacts. They are like the foam that swirls in the bow-wave of a ship, the component bubbles ever drifting back and dissolving in the ship's wake, but the foam always there; old bubbles perpetually being replaced by new as the ship forges on. Cultural artefacts are similar, they express the quasi-mind of the group. These artefacts can be regarded as the imaginative, often frothy, experimentation at the avant-garde or bow-wave of culture as it adapts to changing circumstances: 'moving with the times.' Those creations which catch the mood, the ones which help to give it corporate focus and to refresh the tramlines of society, are recognised as the most valuable.

The point here is that retrospect often adjusts these valuations. This observation confirms Ernst Meyer's reminder that behaviour is the pacemaker of evolution, (see the Cooperate-or-split dilemma in PART 2). It explains culture as an 'adaptive' or genetically stable function of survival and prosperity. Without culture to pin down best *group* practices, we would be doomed to continually reinventing the wheel. So rather surprisingly here lies a direct connection between the froth of contemporary art and the biological remorselessness of natural selection.

This connection may be considered a useful spin-off; an illumination shone by assembly and performance thinking. The value of cultural artefacts lies in how well they contribute to the laying down of cultural tramlines. They do this by mirroring our group quasi-mind back to us. Museums are essentially hallowed places where we can tune in to the quasi-mind of the particular society on show This criterion may help art critics and collectors to assess the quality and monetary value of past and present cultural artefacts. Cultural artefacts express our self-image, and always have.

What I am suggesting is that if you want to collect the artefacts of today which will hold their value in the future and even make millions one day, it is good advice to go for those which are best at both capturing and reflecting like a mirror the self-image of the times. Art, even rebellious graffiti, by expressing the social mood of the times for all to see thus contributes to the business of laying down cultural tramlines. This holds as true of ancient cave paintings and Neolithic religious figurines, of ancient Egyptian art, ancient Greek graffiti, European medieval cathedral architecture, Moroccan arabesque and the stodgy paintings produced in stodgy Napoleonic France as it does right up to the 'conceptual' offerings of today, from the French Impressionists to the wonderful confusion, the froth, that surrounds us now. This is the froth that has been ever changing but always there since Neolithic times This observation can never be a magic formula for getting rich quick, but it may be useful as a definition or standard of measurement for the average citizen trying to make sense of the bewildering froth-confusion of the contemporary art market. This has always been true of art; it doesn't only apply to today's art scene.

God: The Group Quasi-Mind, Is Indispensable; Atheism Unworkable

J. H. Robb says that Emile Durkheim recognised God as the personification of the group quasi-mind:

> Durkheim recognised the existence of a great and powerful influence over human life. This influence he believed was society itself and in worshipping divine beings humans are effectively acknowledging their dependence on society, symbolising this especially in the rituals of worship. The reality of the importance of society provides a basis for the reality of religion.
>
> J. H. Robb, *The Emergence of Social Theory*, op.cit., page 120.

Robb goes on to quote Durkheim's conclusion:

'In reality then, there are no religions which are false. All are true in their own fashion, all answer, though in different ways, to the given conditions of human existence.'

Emile Durkheim, *Elementary Forms*, op.cit., page 3.

A group is always motivated by ambition, it always has a purpose, and that purpose is what triggered its assembly in the first place, conjuring up its quasi-mind. Thus, the quasi-mind comes into being at the assembly stage. It is not one of the group's three navigation functions or parameters: plan > act > review >. Instead it presides over the group, prioritising and orchestrating its conflicting imperatives to metabolise, self-protect or breed and ensuring the continual iteration of its feedback control loop.

God can thus be defined as the personification – the turning into a person – of the quasi-mind of society.

The reasoning goes as follows: humans form social hierarchies in which bigger and bigger political groupings are amalgamated from family to village, village to local authority and from there on up to kingdom. Each has its own quasi-mind, but each level acknowledges the superiority of the one above. At successive levels this quasi-mind is personified in its leadership, and decked out with honorific titles, banners and uniforms whose heroic status and splendour rises in ever increasing steps. This escalates until the invention of God, seen as the highest imaginable, supernatural, social regulator becomes irresistible. St Anselm, a medieval monk, used this sort of reasoning to prove the existence of God, it is referred to in philosophy as 'the ontological argument'. Robert Graves explored this crescendo in *The White Goddess* (1986); it's the crescendo which enthrones God as the symbolic summit of a tribe or nation. And nations cannot organise themselves without some form of communal unifying principle.

This enables us to describe the nature of God in more detail. If God is the personification of the group quasi-mind it follows that both should have similar mental capacities. And indeed, they are very similar; both use irrational emotion alongside reason to impose their will. As Gustave Le Bon pointed out, groups are often quite stupid. The mental capacities we attribute to our gods are on a par with those of an orca pod or wolf pack. The emotions they both deploy include fear, joy, triumph, sadness, self-satisfaction, pride, frenzy, hysteria and shame. The clincher is that both God and the group-mind, carry powerful authority; they increase or reduce our supply of social electricity. And like the conductor of an orchestra they both direct it to specific purposes: feeding, self-protecting or breeding, as necessary to pursue for survival and prosperity. This differential directing of social electricity is the prime function of both God and of the group quasi-mind; they are really the same thing.

This brings atheism into question. Since society yearns to personify its quasi-mind as a figurehead or focal point, it seems unwise to hope that atheism might one day eliminate religion. Mythical revelations of a white, male, bearded God-on-a-throne do of course wander about in fairyland. But if atheism could successfully abolish the recognition of any superhuman authority in whose name we cooperate, it would undermine culture, and with weakened culture a group is vulnerable to takeover. No banner – no *esprit de corps*. In other words, assembly and performance thinking shows that atheism cannot work in real life. That's because, by its own definition, it cannot propose any replacement to the God it has demolished. Any such replacement, humanitarianism for example, would itself become God in a different guise. The name would be different, but the definition would still be *the quasi-mind of the group*.

Social mammals feel compelled to reinforce and consolidate the group quasi-mind. When my dog Rufus comes out walking, the first thing on his mind is to tune in to the canine-scented messages about what is going on in the dog world of our village. Next he reminds it that he's around by urinating on lampposts. The human compulsion to do the same is comprehensively demonstrated by the explosive growth of Facebook, Twitter and other social media. In celebrating our sociability: in reinforcing our group's quasi-mind, we are continually refreshing our image of our corporate selves. Atheism: the absence of this transcendental image will never catch on; something will always be put in its place. It's not just nature that abhors a vacuum, so does society.

Social Power – Who Is the Boss? Who is Running the Show?

According to The Mother's Tale in PART 1 above, it's the women who tell the men what to do. As the saying goes: 'Behind every successful man stands a woman telling him he's wrong.' They do it tactfully though because a man must have his pride, but if he fails, he gets kicked out.

Women, on the other hand are mothers; they're in charge of the home so they can't be kicked out.

That was according to The Mother's Tale. Senior citizens, both men and women, aren't quite so sure. In PART 2 it then became clear that it is the group's quasi-mind that runs the show, and that it does so through iterations, however fast or slow, and at multiple levels, of the mutually trumping feedback control loop. These iterations can happen in a flash or take days to complete, and they operate at different levels of the action-hierarchy from the intimate and temporary right up to the nation state. This analysis of social power is one of the brightest illuminations offered by assembly and performance thinking.

But that's not all. This illumination may indeed answer the question about who is running the show, but it's only about who is in charge of the group's *performance*. The setting of its purpose, for example prioritising between the conflicting demands of acquiring energy, self-protection and reproduction, is different. That is done at the *assembly* stage. For example, if it becomes clear that access to water is now more vital to group survival than protecting the children, then the group's priority needs to be reset. This is not a planning function within the Rule of Three, because both the executive and the review functions must first accept the new purpose. For this priority-change the adjustment necessary amounts to a reassembly, creating a quasi-mind alteration.

So here now we have the full answer as to who is running the show according to assembly and performance thinking:

- First, the purpose to be achieved by group performance is decided during the act of assembly. It is done by those who agreed to divide their labour to get something done. In this process they brought a quasi-mind into existence.

- Second, performances of the three functions, plan > act > review >, are each in turn orchestrated or run by the group's quasi-mind.

The group's purpose and priorities, the 'what's to be done' is decided during assembly; it's decided at the stage when the group was being formed. The 'how it's to be done' is different; that's decided at the 'plan' phase *within* the Rule of Three cycle. That's where progress is compared with purpose and act is specified. These questions are always about the survival-and-prosperity of the group: family, tribe, business, multinational or nation.

Who's Running the Show Repeated in Plain Words

If that answer seems a bit complicated here it is again expressed in more down-to-earth everyday language.

The executive boss, prime minister, chief executive, or whatever 'he' is called, is in charge of the action. This is the job of the rational person, who is typically but by no means always a man. This job is to provide supplies for the nest, to protect it and to enable reproduction. To enable the boss to do this job he/she is given control of the group's property: its land, equipment and money. If things go OK and the group prospers, the boss is honoured, and his/her policies become part of the group's culture. But if things go badly and his/her policies begin to fail, the boss may need to be deposed. In that case the group effectively recreates itself, either calmly according to its cultural rules, or in the more violent catharsis of rebellion. This catharsis can if necessary be brought about by emotion. That's to say by a quasi-mind alteration in which rational argument is overwhelmed by the irrational force of emotion. This force is mobilised by public opinion, typically expressed in the media; that is plan mode. So, the media are not actually running the show, but they express its quasi-mind and can cause the deposition of the boss so as to change group policy.

Thus, the rational male is boss. But the irrational female, using emotion if necessary, tells him what needs to be done; she sets his priorities for him. The interplay between men and women was nicely illustrated by Colonel Hathi, the pompous patriarch in charge of the Pachyderm Parade in Walt Disney's classic *The Jungle Book* (1967): he doesn't really understand matters of emotion, morale and family harmony so he leaves them to his wife Winifred.

Democracy is only one of many ways of running the show. But according to assembly and performance thinking, cooperation and the Rule of Three are the only processes which always have and always will underlie all human social behaviour.

It's only when the smooth running of society is in doubt due to reverse trumping – that's to say rebellion, autocracy or social sclerosis – that the question of power and where it lies becomes interesting.

It's as simple as that, and the question about who is running the show, men or women, follows naturally. Women representing the humanist principle, take the lead in deciding what has to be done, they review and prioritise the threats to family and tribe. Men, who have been strutting about looking important but contributing little, are then given the lead; they perform the action, they do the work. Large numbers get killed in battle and are remembered as heroes, but, except in the case of genocide, that doesn't really matter very much because it's the number of women, not men, that limits population growth. One surviving man can impregnate many women, so the women are the ones who are entrusted to carry the genes.

Until the smooth running of the group starts to wobble, social power is not an issue. As was clear when looking at social reality from a Mother's angle in PART 1, power is not interesting until things begin to go wrong. So, whenever we see the word 'power' being used in sociology, we should substitute 'misuse of power'. Social power on its own is fairly meaningless.

Of course, this stuff is highly abstract but so, as I say, is the process of evolution by natural selection. The smooth iteration of the loop is what's essential for group survival in this competitive world.

Structure/Agency Resolved by the Rule of Three

The structure/agency question is about how do little you and me fit into the great institutions of society? how do individuals like us interact with the daunting structure of society? which controls which? This question still bedevils sociology today; big reputations have been made and damaged in its name.

In 1975 Thomas Bottomore phrased the question as follows:

> The real problem is to formulate a conception of social structure
> which does justice to these elements [structure and agency]
> of regularity and order in social life, while not neglecting the
> flow of historical action by individuals and social groups
> which sustains, recreates, revises, or disrupts this order.
> (Bryant 1995, p. 57)

While the Industrial Revolution was gathering pace, eighteenth-century European scholars proposed the study of society as a distinct science. The expectation was that society could be explained by the 'positivistic' methods of natural science. First Auguste Comte and then Emile

Durkheim became the leaders in this movement. But critics then pointed out that their findings were indifferent to the de-humanising effect of mass industrialisation: to the turmoil of change from agrarian to urban living.

So then Max Weber, Georg Simmel and others explored the possibility of a social science focused instead on the individual or 'agent'. One of their ideas was Weber's *verstehen* which translates roughly as understanding a situation from the other person's point of view.

This counter movement frequently suffered from infiltration by unscientific, humanitarian, 'normative', value-judgements. Karl Marx's dialectics, originally Georg Hegel's, and his analysis of capitalism aimed at first to be scientifically positivistic or objective, but later he did little to oppose socialist/proletarian interpretations of his work; he did not attempt to bridge the structure/agency gap. Talcott Parsons tried impressively to integrate structure and agency as social determinants with his 'structural functionalism', but Parsons concentrated on what society is, not on what it does; he worked on society as a phenomenon, not a tool for living. Parsons' AGIL lists group attributes which he said will always emerge spontaneously as consequences of cooperation. They are merely descriptive. Other structure/agency attempts include Anthony Giddens's *Structuration Theory* (1984) which is a useful re-statement of the dilemma but is somewhat inconclusive. Pierre Bourdieu proposed the twin concepts of *habitus*, very similar to the personal mental library of social responses (see Cooperate-or-split PART 2 above), and *field*, similar to the ever-changing array of cooperating groups described in the raindrop rings metaphor, (see PART 2 above). As with structuration theory, Bourdieu's generic structuralism is a lucid description of the two-way relations between structure and agency.

But without dynamic processes, descriptions don't amount to mechanisms. Mechanisms have to be set ticking. What we need are explanations, not just definitions or descriptions of working parts.

When scholars start to get bogged down in the interconnections between two already abstract concepts – in this case structure and agency – it's probably time to regress: to go back through those Russian dolls, and review the first principles on which the whole debate is founded. That's to say how does society's mechanism work? Assembly and performance thinking are about just that: the dynamics of the mechanism of society.

Assembly and performance thinking introduces three mutually trumping, constantly iterating elements instead of the two recognised in structure/agency scholarship. In this way the whole question is side-stepped or dissolved, it becomes a non-question.

The claim here is that assembly and performance thinking dissolves the structure/agency dichotomy in the following way:

- Genetically socialisable mammals notice a threat or opportunity and sense a quorum.

- They switch mode from selfish individual to cog in an assembled group in which labour is divided, and they readily subordinate their individual advantages to the will of the group quasi-mind. There's your structure.

- This assembled group performs its purpose as a unit, iterating the loop. Its plan > execute > review > navigation parameters are mutually trumping, just as they are in a solitary animal. And there's your agency.

- The group performs, spawning mini groups as it grows. These naturally arrange themselves in a rough-and-tumble social hierarchy. Together they make up society.

- Instead of a structure/agency dichotomy, individuals or 'agents' are integrated, as cogs in a machine. Its mutual trumping progresses as the work of the group gets done.

- Reverse trumping, lubricated by emotion, can destroy a group, and if this happens and there is a new quorum, a new group can be assembled.

The agreed purpose of assembled individuals, or *agents*, focuses the group's quasi-mind. In performance these individuals are coordinated, or *structured*, by cultural tramlines. Following the Rule of Three, as in target shooting, they plan, they execute, and then, in review, they register progress, automatically adjusting their cultural tramlines in this process. Then they plan what to do next; and so on; round and round the loop. Cooperation can degenerate into autocracy, rebellion or sclerosis. When that happens, the problem may be diagnosed as a failure either of assembly or of loop iteration and, like a sick patient, the group may be treated accordingly.

In this model the structure/agency problem becomes a non-problem. It turns into a triangular arrangement. The structure/agency dilemma, an intellectual concept, is dissolved in the mechanism of group assembly and performance, another intellectual concept.

CONCLUSION

A Universal Mechanism

Human groups include families, tribes and businesses as well as multinationals and nation states. Together they comprise the hierarchy of society. I have tried to say that purposeful human groups always function according to a universal mechanism, referred to as assembly and performance thinking, and that this same mechanism is used by all cooperating mammals. This way of thinking is not meant to be a description of static components or a 'naming of parts'; instead, I have tried to explain the dynamic workings of society; the way its cogs turn.

This thinking amounts to a unified set of thoughts and principles about how human society works. It even applies, with suitable variations which have been explained by Stuart West, E. O. Wilson and others, to all cooperating animals, including microbes.

Society is still an enigma. Good behaviour is taught in every home and yet we are constantly going to war. Genocide is common, and we humans seem unable to prevent ourselves from polluting the land and sea. We keep killing each other and fouling our own nest.

Several recent ideas have brought us to the brink of a scientific explanation of how human society works. These include Darwin's natural selection, Weiner's cybernetics, Parsons's AGIL, Durkheim's objectivity and his 'reverse trumping', Gustave Le Bon's 'crowd', Lewin's spiral, Wilfred Bion's group therapy, E. O. Wilson's socio-biology, W. D. Hamilton's rule of relatedness, and Pierre Bourdieu's field and *habitus*. I have tried to show how these ideas might be brought together as the components of a scientific explanation of human society.

This way of thinking may be new but it's not rocket-science; it may need a second reading, but it is simple and requires no prior knowledge of sociology; it needs no mathematics, statistics or ethics. It comes in two layers of thought. The first observes the formation of cooperating groups, which in evolutionary biology is not an easy achievement. These groups are unified living organisms assembled to perform one, two, or all of life's functions. Delving deeper, the second layer reveals how every group performs by cycling through three mutually trumping trial-and-error functions: these are like the parlour game 'scissors, paper and stone'. This rule is not rigid; it is an optimum, like advising an opening batsman to keep his bat straight; it is good practice but not compulsory.

Then comes the twist: reverse trumping, lubricated by emotion, can destroy a group. At that stage if there is still a life-function job to be done, and if there is a new quorum willing to do it, then a new group can be assembled, rising like the phoenix out of the ashes.

The Fog of Hubris

Assembly and performance thinking is not difficult, so the first question has to be why wasn't it noticed many centuries ago? The answer offered here is hubris; the great fallacy of self-importance which was so powerfully promoted by Plato in 400BC. When we think of ourselves privately as individuals, we seldom consider ourselves to be significant. But any group we belong to has a purpose, and the common pursuit of this purpose engenders a shared sense of self-importance: a belief in ourselves which can be 'personified' in many different ways. As compatriots we are proudly confident in the importance of 'ourselves'. But this corporate sense of hubris, hangs over us. Like fog on a landscape, it presides over our corporate quasi-mind. It whispers that we are supreme amongst God's creations, rulers of the earth. We cannot see our true nature as one of the social mammals until this fog rolls away. Then we may find it easier to discern the mechanism of society, and to establish how it works.

Assembly and Performance Thinking in a Nutshell

1. The human is one of many animals, microbes to mammals, which, despite Darwin's natural selfishness, have managed to evolve the altruism necessary for cooperation.

2. So, when something needs to be done, we are able to *assemble* into a purposeful working group which is more effective than the total of its individuals' efforts.

3. The group's purpose is driven by the ambition to survive and prosper; this always boils down to acquiring energy, ensuring self-protection or breeding, or combinations of these.

4. The assembled group then *performs* its purpose, iterating cyclically through three mutually trumping 'trial-and-error' functions: > review > plan > act. This is called a cybernetic feedback control loop, referred to here as 'the Rule of Three'. It is the $e = mc^2$ equivalent of assembly and performance thinking.

5. This rational thinking only wields a weak social force, and when a crisis hits, the strong force of emotion can disrupt a group and even destroy it. In that case if a new quorum exists, then a new group can emerge.

Society is still as enigmatic as it was in Plato's day. Actually, it's worse than that because the rudder's now gone. We have abandoned the usually humanising dogma of religion without having anything better than political correctness to put in its place. And we are drifting towards a frightening vision of runaway global warming. We are fouling our own nest. We urgently need to understand how society works. A good way to start could be to banish our preening hubris so that we can examine the mechanism of assembly and performance.

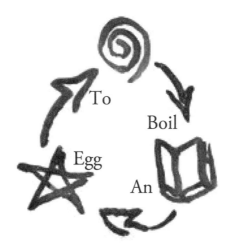

My Thanks . . .

It is an ancient mariner,
And he stoppeth one of three,
By thy long grey beard and glittering eye,
Now wherefore Stopp'st thou me?

It has taken me twenty-three long years to research the ideas in this book. Throughout this time, I have frequently felt like Samuel Taylor Coleridge's grey-beard loon. I have bored the pants off innumerable people; oldest and closest friends, colleagues, many of my personal heroes, academics and casual acquaintances. Sadly, several key critics and sounding boards including John Gibson himself have died since I started. But it is perfectly clear that I could never possibly have developed this Assembly and Performance thinking without you all, so I am immensely grateful, and I thank you, each one, most humbly.

A. C. B. Wilson. August 30, 2020

BIBLIOGRAPHY & REFERENCES

Abrutyn, Seth (2016) *Handbook of Contemporary Sociological Theory*, Switzerland: Springer.

Apicella, C et al. *Social Networks and Cooperation in Hunter-gatherers*, Nature, 26/1/2012.

Archer, M. (2007) *Making Our Way Through the World*, Cambridge University Press.

Archer, M. (2010) *Morphogenesis Versus Structuration*, British Journal of Sociology, 33.

Beck, U. (2010) *Varieties of Second Modernity: The Cosmopolitan Turn in Social and Political Theory and Research*, British Journal of Sociology, 61.

Bhaskar, R. (1979) *The Possibility of Naturalism*, Sussex: Harvester.

Bion, W. (1996) *Experiences in Groups*, London: Routledge.

Bray, D. (2011) *Wetware: A Computer in Every Living Cell*, Yale University Press.

Bryant, C. (1995) *Practical Sociology*, Cambridge: Polity Press.

Buckley, W. (1967) *Sociology and Modern Systems Theory*, New Jersey: Prentice-Hall.

Calhoun, C. et al. (2002) *Classical Sociological Theory*, Oxford: Basil Blackwell.

Clayton, Ewan (2019) *Writing: Making your Mark*, London: The British Library.

Cornford, F. M. (1937) *Plato's Cosmology*, Indiana: Hackett Publishing Co. Inc.

Corning, P. (2005) *Holistic Darwinism*, Chicago: The University of Chicago Press.

Darwin, C. (1968) *The Origin of Species*, Penguin Classics.

Darwin, C. (2004) *The Descent of Man*, London: Penguin Classics.

De Waal, F. (2006) *The Animal Roots of Human Morality*, New Scientist, Oct 2006.

De Waal, F. et al. (2006) *Self-recognition in an Asian Elephant*, Proceedings of the National Academy of Sciences, 103 no. 45.

Dodds, E. R. (1951) *The Greeks and the Irrational*, University of California Press.

Durkheim, Emile (1893) *The Division of Labour in Society*, London: Palgrave.

Durkheim, Emile (1912) *The Elementary Forms of Religious Life*, Oxford World Classics.

Giddens, A. (1984) *The Constitution of Society*, Cambridge: Polity.

Gramsci, A. (2005) *Selections from the Prison Notebooks*, London: Lawrence & Wishart.

Graves, R. (1986) *The White Goddess*, London: Faber & Faber.

Hammersley, M. (2010) *The Case of the Disappearing Dilemma: Herbert Blumer on Sociological Method*, History of the Human Sciences, 23 (5).

Hamilton, W. D. (1964) *The Genetical Evolution of Social Behaviour*, Journal of Theoretical Biology, 7.

Harari, Y. N. (2011) Sapiens – *A Brief History of Humankind*, London: Vintage.

Hardin, G. (1968) *The Tragedy of the Commons*, Science 162.

Haw, M. (2012) *DNA dynamos*, Nature 491.

Holldobler, B. and Wilson E. (2008) *The Superorganism: The beauty, elegance and strangeness of insect societies*, New York: W. W. Norton.

Keneally, T. (1982) *Schindler's Ark*, London: Hodder and Stoughton.

Kenny, A. (2001) *A Brief History of Western Philosophy*, Oxford: Blackwell.

King, A. (2004) *The Structure of Social Theory*, London: Routledge.

King, A. (2010) *The Afghan War and 'Postmodern' Memory: Commemoration and the Dead of Helmand*, British Journal of Sociology, 61.

King, A. and de Rond, M. (2011) *Boat Race: Rhythm and the Possibility of Collective Performance*, British Journal of Sociology, 62.

Le Bon, Gustave. (1896) *The Crowd*, New York: Dover.

Machiavelli, N. (1961) *The Prince*, London: Penguin Classics.

Mandeville, B. (1989) *The Fable of the Bees*, London: Penguin Classics.

Marcouse, Ian et al. (2015) *AQA Business of A Level*, London: Hodder Education.

Mautner, T. ed (2000) *The Penguin Dictionary of Philosophy*, London: Penguin Classics.

McClelland, K. and Fararo, T. (2006) *Purpose, Meaning, and Action*, New York: Palgrave.

Meyer, E. (2001) *What Evolution Is*, New York: Basic Books.

Montesquieu, de (1748) *The Spirit of the Laws*, trs.1989: Cambridge University Press.

Morris, G. (1969) *Montesquieu and the Varieties of Political Experience*, Pelican Books.

Patterson, L. (1991) *Chaucer & the Subject of History*, University of Wisconsin Press.

Parsons, T. (1937) *The Structure of Social Action*, New York: McGraw-Hill.

Powers, W. (1973) *Behaviour: The Control of Perception*, Chicago: Aldine.

Robb, J. H. (2001) *The Emergence of Social Theory*, Wellington, N.Z: Astra Print Ltd.

Robert III, H. M. (1876) *Robert's Rules of Order* (11th Edition, 1970): Da Capo Press USA.

Robinson, D. (2007) *Control theories in Sociology*, Annual Review of Sociology, 33.

Rocher, Guy. (1974) *Talcott Parsons and American Sociology*, Nashville: Thomas Nelson.

Rousseau, J. J. (2007) *The Social Contract*, London: Penguin Classics.

Sumner, W. (1906) *Folkways*, Boston: Ginn and Co.

Swingewood, A. (2000) *A Short History of Sociological Thought*, London: Palgrave.

Tawnay, R. H. (1926) *Religion and the Rise of Capitalism*, London: Routledge.

Topitsch, E. (1971) *Max Weber and Sociology Today* (ed. Stammer) Oxford: Blackwell.

Tuomela, R. (2007) *The Philosophy of Sociality*, Oxford University Press.

Turner, J. H. (2001) *Handbook of Contemporary Sociological Theory*, Springer-Verlag US.

Weber, M. (1922) *Economy and Society*, University of California Press.

Weber, M. (1949) *The Methodology of the Social Sciences*, New York: Free Press.

West, S. et al. (2007) *Evolutionary Explanations for Cooperation*, Current Biology, 17.

Wiener, N. (1948) *Cybernetics or Control and Communication in the Animal and the Machine*, New York: Wiley.

Wilson, Tony (A. C. B.) (2007) *The Universe on a Bicycle*, London, Elliott & Thompson.

Wilson, D. S. (2002) *Darwin's Cathedral*, University of Chicago Press.

Wilson, E. O. (2000) *Sociobiology*, Harvard University Press.

Wright, M. R. (1997) *Routledge History of Philosophy*, Volume 1. London.